MONTANA
ENTERTAINERS

FAMOUS AND ALMOST FORGOTTEN

MONTANA

ENTERTAINERS

FAMOUS AND ALMOST FORGOTTEN

Brian D'Ambrosio

THE
History
PRESS

Published by The History Press
Charleston, SC
www.historypress.com

Front cover: Top left, Montie Montana; top right, Chief Many Treaties; middle left, Julian Eltinge; middle right, Mary MacLane; bottom left, Shane Clouse; bottom right, Walter Coy. *Back cover*: Top, Marliza Pons; bottom, Charley Pride.

First published 2019

Manufactured in the United States

ISBN 9781467141109

Library of Congress Control Number: 2019936988

With great love to Sophia, the darling entertainer and performer and all-around incredible kid; to Monkey, my loving mom; to Dad, enjoy the loveliness of each new day; to the memory of Veronica Mavencamp

CONTENTS

ACKNOWLEDGEMENTS

Special thanks to Rossah Bendahman, for the information about Marliza Pons; Troy Bertelsen, for the memories of Steve Reeves; Dirk Benedict; Bill Bowers; Jeff Bridges; the Buffalo Bill Center of the West; Tom Catmull; Shane Clouse; Jason DeShaw; Mark Guerrero; John W. Heap, for his memories of the Coburn family; Robbie Knievel; Colin Meloy; Charley Pride; Chan Romero; the Silent Era Film Association, Zoe Anne Stoltz and the good people of the Montana Historical Society for their enthusiasm and research; Reggie Watts; and George Winston.

INTRODUCTION

At age eighty-five, a ranch girl from Montana was honored at the Academy Awards on March 25, 1991. From humble beginnings, Myrna Loy grew up with culture, near Helena, to become a screen legend and cultural icon in the 1930s for her role as the witty Nora Charles in the *Thin Man* movies. She was reported to have been President Franklin Roosevelt's favorite actress. Gangster John Dillinger was watching one of her films when he was tracked down and killed by G-men in Chicago's Biograph Theater.

But Loy wasn't the first or the last Montana product to reap stage or entertainment success. Indeed, from Butte native Pert Kelton, whose name shined in the lights of old Broadway and who was the first actress who played Alice Kramden in the original "The Honeymooners" with Jackie Gleason, to Andrea Leeds, the daughter of an English mining engineer, nominated for a Best Supporting Actress Oscar in 1937 for the film *Stage Door*, Montana's invasion of Cinemaland, television studio lots and music venues began more than 125 years ago.

To be sure, many Montanans have beat a path from way up there in the North to way down there in the warmth of California, making it the trail to cinema success—recognizing that for all the achievements of regional theater, New York and Los Angeles were, or perhaps still are, where the big money and reputations are made: Kathlyn Williams, Gary Cooper, Myrna Loy, Helen Lynch, Lane Chandler, Fritzi Ridgeway, Barbara Luddy, Wallace and Dorothy

Coburn, Kay Hammond, Julian Eltinge and Doris Deane Arbuckle. And that's only part of the list.

While many found unparalleled success during the Golden Age of Hollywood, for every Cooper and Loy, there is someone who was more typical of the type of actors that appeared in movies throughout Hollywood's history. Ward Ramsey, of Helena, was one of innumerable supporting players who backed those who headlined the films and made them memorable. Ramsey has the merit of being one of the few who have battled dinosaurs and lived to speak about it (in the 1960 film *Dinosaurus!*).

For every Gary Cooper, there are two unheralded Stanley Andersons, a Billings-born character actor, who for decades played the young, the mature, the brazen, the bashful, the callous, the tender, the swaggering and the impotent, or one contemporarily overlooked Steve Reeves, a native son of the Richland community in northeastern Montana, international film star, bodybuilder and Mr. America of 1947 who gained fame portraying characters like Hercules and Ulysses in the Italian spectaculars of the late 1950s and early 1960s.

Talent, like gold, is where you find it. For more than 125 years, Montana has supplied a rich vein of entertainment and personality, such as George Montgomery, from Brady, who made a slew of westerns in the 1930s and later musicals and detective films. While Montgomery achieved a moderate amount of success in his time, others studiously pieced together careers through constant application. Helena-born James C. Morton was a supporting actor who made nearly two hundred films between the 1920s and 1940s; Thomas Wilson, also from Helena, played mostly bit parts through his fifty-year career, including a mustachioed policeman in Charlie Chaplin's *The Kid* (1921).

Yes, we've sent plenty of Montanans off to appear as "western" stars, including Walter Darwin Coy, who made several films, including *The Searchers* with John Wayne, but found prolific work in television making westerns, and Ethan Allen Laidlaw, from Butte, gainfully employed in Hollywood between the 1920s and 1960s. A prolific small-part actor in westerns, Laidlaw appeared in literally hundreds of pictures often as a gruff, bearded henchman, pirate or gang member.

Some of our connections are as irresistibly sweet as sorghum molasses. Kathryn Card was born in Butte and is best known for being the voice of Lucy's mother on *I Love Lucy*. Card thus connects to Lucille Ball, the daughter of a lineman in Anaconda and elsewhere in Montana and who would become the country's most famous comedienne and truly a television pioneer. While it's a delicious rumor to contemplate (though impossible to corroborate), "Uncle Dick" Sutton, who made Butte the best show town in the West before relocating to California and was once referred to "as one of the most remarkable and memorable personages in American show history," is purported in Montana theatrical lore to be the one who advised Al Jolson to don blackface and thus march to great success. That tidbit allegedly was passed on in the days when Al was working the theater circuit in Butte.

For more than thirty years, the former Montana ranch boy Clarence Sinclair Bull headed the still photo department of Metro-Goldwyn-Mayer Studios, the only man for whom Greta Garbo would pose for a photographic portrait. He bought his first camera at Murphy-Maclay Hardware Company in Great Falls with the money earned by selling magazines on horseback and bicycle in the Sun River country. His dreamlike photographic images of MGM stars such as Garbo, Hedy Lamarr and Katharine Hepburn were instrumental in setting the standards of beauty to this day. One of our connections was so famous she was nominally known by her first name, "Irene." Beginning her Hollywood career as an actress playing ingénue parts opposite Mack Sennett's leading comedians, Baker native Irene Lentz was nominated for the Academy Award for Best Costume Design, Black-and-White, for *B.F.'s Daughter* (1948) and Best Costume Design, Color, for *Midnight Lace* (1960). Her designs were reputed to be the first featured at a boutique devoted to a single designer inside a major U.S. store.

The contribution of Montanans to the performing or theatrical arts is by no means relegated to one genre. Michael Smuin, the son of a Safeway butcher born in Missoula, took tap and ballet lessons as a child and at fourteen qualified to study dance at the University of Utah, where he was spotted by the director of the San Francisco Ballet. For decades, Smuin (1938–2007) wowed audiences as a Broadway and ballet choreographer with a physically powerful sense of craft.

Our famous and almost forgotten are a curious and diverse lot. Some of them, such as Hazel Warp, worked discreetly. Warp, a Sweet Grass County native who became a rodeo trick rider in her teens, stood in for Vivien Leigh in all the horseback riding scenes in 1939's *Gone with the Wind*. She even took a tumble for Leigh, falling down the stairs of Tara in the famous scene toward the end of the film when Scarlett reaches out to slap Rhett Butler, loses her balance and falls. Onetime Butte resident Julian

Eltinge went on to become America's first famous female impersonator. There was Taylor Gordon, whose golden voice propelled the son of a slave from White Sulphur Springs to fame. And Marysville's Frank James "Brownie" Burke went from working as a bellhop at Yellowstone Park's Mammoth Hot Springs Hotel to entertaining fans as the mascot of the Cincinnati Reds baseball team.

Some entertainers, such as country music legend Charley Pride, developed their talents here and then moved on to greatness. Pride's music career began in Montana in 1960 during a time when he played professional baseball for teams in East Helena and Missoula. As a sideline, Pride crooned in local nightclubs in Helena and Great Falls, where he attracted the attention of country artist Red Sovine.

Other entertainers were born here either via coincidence or downright accident or lived here extremely briefly, such as Martha Raye, who was born in Butte during a stopover on her parents' vaudeville tour on August 27, 1916. She began acting at age three, attended schools in Chicago and New York and grew up onstage in theaters, vaudeville shows and nightclubs. Her resounding voice and wide grin made her a favorite on the entertainment circuit. By the 1950s, she was hosting her own highly rated television show, reaching millions with her clowning.

Still others laid down roots here at the pinnacle of their careers, such as Pablo Elvira, a Puerto Rico–born baritone who became a regular member of the New York City Opera in the 1970s and '80s and sang frequently with the Metropolitan Opera. He moved to Montana after finding success and considered it home.

Several retained longer, deeper, lifetime affiliations, such as Chet Huntley, whose journey from the Hi-Line to the "big time" as a newscaster began in a one-room schoolhouse that stands refurbished near Saco. Actor Carroll O'Connor met his wife, Nancy, at the university after World War II and returned to Missoula in the summer of 2000, when Carroll taught two enormously popular sections called "Writing the Movie."

Some of our connections are still considerably famous (like Gary Cooper and Charley Pride), some were full of character and color yet were never quite famous (Red Lodge–born Jane Drummond claimed a stunning screen presence, yet she never reached the upper echelon of her chosen profession) and others were famous yet are almost forgotten today, such as Wallace Coburn (1872–1954), northern Montana's original cowboy poet and movie star, or Pee Wee Holmes, a diminutive silent-era film star who made it from eastern Montana to Hollywood stardom as a slapstick sidekick.

Each entertainer serves as a testament to the universality of dreams and the idea that success comes to those who eschew barriers and borders and apply their talents with vigor and excitement.

BORN BETWEEN 1875 AND 1910

ROBYN ADAIR

Born February 11, 1884, Miles City, Montana
Died February 16, 1965

Born in Miles City in 1884, actor Robyn Adair is a near-complete stranger to movie historians, which is hard to fathom considering he appeared as everything from prospector to shady casino owner to railroad conductor to tramp telegrapher in at least 113 films between 1912 and 1917. Sometimes appearing under the name J. Robyn Adair, he is most notable for his roles in *A Romance of the Sea* (1914), *Across the Desert* (1915) and *The Honor of the Camp* (1915). While other film sources, including IMDb, note Adair's birth year as 1884, Billy Doyle's book *The Ultimate Dictionary of the Silent Screen Performers* claims that he was born in Miles City, Montana, in 1885 but lists no death date or year. According to Doyle, Adair was a "film pioneer," as he started making one- and two-reel action and western shorts in 1912. He also appeared in six features in 1916–17.

Doris Deane Arbuckle
(Born Doris Anita Dibble)

Born January 20, 1900, Wisconsin
Died March 24, 1974, Hollywood, California

Born in Wisconsin in 1900, Doris Anita Dibble was the daughter of a man who, among other miscellaneous career attempts, manufactured and sold musical instruments. As Doris was a child of two peripatetic parents, in 1910 her family were renting a house in Iowa, where her father worked in a saloon, but by her high school years they were living in Butte (several sources incorrectly provide her birthplace in Butte in 1900). After leaving Butte, she lived in New York and Chicago before her family moved to Pasadena, California. There she finished her schooling before she returned to New York to dance with the Mary Morgan troupe.

After playing small parts in several J. Stuart Blackton movies in New York, Doris went west again. Under the alias Doris Deane, she made films for MGM, Universal and, from 1923 to 1925, on the Buster Keaton lot, including *His First Car* (1924), *Stupid, But Brave* (1924) and *Dynamite Doggie* (1925). It was while working for Keaton that she and Roscoe Conkling "Fatty" Arbuckle, a disgraced silent film–era performer, fell in love.

In 1921, Arbuckle was arrested in San Francisco for the rape and murder of aspiring actress Virginia Rappe. Many felt that he was used as a scapegoat by religious and moral reformer Will Hays for the troubles and excesses of Hollywood. (Hays, chairman of the Motion Picture Association of America from 1922 to 1945, became the namesake of the 1930 Motion Picture Production Code, informally referred to as the Hays Code, which spelled out a set of moral guidelines for the self-censorship of content in Hollywood cinema.) Arbuckle was later acquitted by a jury, but the scandal daggered his career.

In 1925, Doris and "Fatty" married. Arbuckle had divorced his first wife only a few months earlier, and he had been carrying the crushing stress of the three trials (between November 1921 and April 1922) he had to endure with the Rappe scandal.

At the time of their marriage, Arbuckle, a post-scandal outsider of the motion picture industry, found himself unemployable as an actor and rapidly descending into heavy alcohol abuse. Arbuckle and Deane divorced in 1928.

It was while working for Buster Keaton that Doris Dibble and Roscoe Conkling "Fatty" Arbuckle, a disgraced silent era performer, fell in love. They were married in 1925 and divorced within three years. *Courtesy Butte Archives.*

Doris, who appeared in a short titled *Marriage Rows* in 1931 and last appeared in television or film in 1951, died on March 24, 1974, in Hollywood.

The *Montana Standard* in 1924 provided this generous fragment: "Doris Deane Arbuckle—Doris Dibble at Butte and a member of one of the best known families there—as pretty a girl ever graced the city of the richest hill on earth. It didn't surprise the home folk to learn she was on the success pathway."

DOROTHY (DODDS) BAKER

Born April 21, 1907, Missoula, Montana
Died June 17, 1968, Terra Bella, California

Daughter of Raymond Branson Dodds and Alice Grady, Dorothy Dodds was born in Missoula in 1907. Wife of literary critic Howard Baker, Dorothy was a novelist and actress, known for writing *Young Man with a Horn* (1950) and *Playhouse 90* (1956). California-raised and a graduate of UCLA, after tinkering with a few experimental short stories, she turned to writing full time; in 1938, she published the novel *Young Man with a Horn*, which was inspired by the life of Bix Beiderbecke, a cornet player who reached Jazz Age superstardom before sinking into alcoholism and dying in 1931 at age twenty-eight. Warner Bros. adapted the musical drama in 1950, casting Kirk Douglas as Rick Martin, a tormented trumpeter who suffers through a ruinous marriage with an angst-stricken socialite before being redeemed by another's love. Dorothy acted in few television shows in the mid-1950s, but evidently her talent and career was as a writer. She continued to write novels up until the time of her death in 1968 of cancer.

DIANE BORI

Born September 17, 1910, Butte, Montana
Died September 14, 2004, Santa Monica, California

Born in Butte, Diane Bori acted in several films in the 1930s, most notably as Etheline in *Big Town* (1932) starring Lester Vail, and the drama *Ann Carver's Profession* (1933), featuring Fay Wray. Bori died on September 14, 2004, in Santa Monica, California.

ROBERT BRAY

Born October 23, 1917, Kalispell, Montana
Died March 7, 1983, Bishop, California

Bray was born to homesteading parents in Kalispell. According to a 1936 certificate of the Register of the Land Office at Kalispell, Robert's father, Oliver J. Bray, made full payment for "the Southwest Quarter of Section

Kalispell-born Robert Bray entered films in 1946 under contract to RKO. Similar to other young, handsome talents, he was marketed as the "next Gary Cooper." Bray appeared as private detective Mike Hammer in the 1957 film noir crime thriller *My Gun Is Quick. Courtesy Flathead Valley Historical Society.*

Twenty-One in Township Twenty-Four North of Range Twenty-Three West of the Montana Meridian, Montana, Containing One Hundred Sixty Acres." By 1920, Oliver was employed as shoe salesman, and the family of five resided in "Kalispell Ward 3," on South Main Street.

The Brays moved to Seattle's East Sixty-Eighth Street, and Robert attended Lincoln High School. After graduation, he was a lumberjack, a cowboy and a member of the Civilian Conservation Corps. In 1942, Bray joined the United States Marine Corps and saw action in the South Pacific during World War II, finishing his enlistment ranked master sergeant.

Bray entered films in 1946 under contract to RKO. Similar to other handsome young talents, he was marketed as the "next Gary Cooper." While he never attained the stardom of Montana-born Cooper, Bray appeared in B westerns like 1949's *Rustlers*. In the 1950s, the freelancing actor appeared in a varied number of television roles. While he starred in *The Lone Ranger* and *Stagecoach West*, Bray is perhaps most remembered for his role as the forest ranger Corey Stuart in the later seasons of the long-running CBS series *Lassie*.

From 1964 to 1969, Bray played the role of the forest ranger who was one of Lassie's last masters in the series, which ran from 1954 to 1970.

He died at his home at age sixty-five, survived by his wife and six children.

FRANCESCA BRUNING

Born March 13, 1907, Miles City, Montana
Died November 1996, New York City, New York

Most noted as a stage actress, Francesca Bruning also appeared in a pair of television shows in the 1940s, which seems to be the full extent of her television and film career: *The Ford Theatre Hour* (1948) and *The Big Story* (1949). Interestingly, there is a collection in New York City of Francesa Bruning's family papers documenting her family history and her early life. The bulk of the material is letters from her father, Dr. L.C. Bruning, a county health officer in Custer County, Montana, to her mother, Ruby Bruning (née Houg). A letter Dr. Bruning wrote in 1898 while serving in the U.S. military in the Philippines is also present. Ruby Bruning held property in Custer County and Powder River County, Montana, and the family papers include title abstracts and other documents regarding the property and mortgages between 1914 and 1927. Pictures of Bruning's family and childhood, as well as some pictures from her early career, are held with the family papers. The earliest items in the collection are photographic portraits from the 1860s and an invitation to Bruning's grandmother's wedding, dated 1875.

CLARENCE SINCLAIR BULL

Born 1896, Sun River, Montana
Died June 8, 1979, Los Angeles, California

For more than thirty years, the former Montana ranch boy headed the still photo department of Metro-Goldwyn-Mayer Studios. He was the only man for whom Greta Garbo would pose for a photographic portrait.

Bull's grandfather Charles A. Bull was a pioneer of the Sun River country west of Great Falls. He came to Montana Territory and the new town of Sun River in 1867 from Indiana. Bull's father, also named Charles A. Bull, was born in 1874 at Sun River, where Clarence Bull was born in 1896.

"My grandfather had a sort of trading post," recalled Bull in his biography, *The Man Who Shot Garbo*. "It was in this building that the Rev. W.W. Van Orsdel [the circuit-riding Methodist known widely as "Brother Van"] conducted his first services in Sun River in June, 1872."

Bull's father went to school in Sun River, and later his grandmother sent him to study law at the University of Michigan. While in Michigan, the younger Charles A. Bull met and married Belle Sinclair, a Scotch-Canadian schoolteacher. When he graduated, they moved west and stayed on the Bull ranch at Sun River. Several years after Clarence Bull's birth, his parents moved to another Bull ranch east of Cascade, on the Missouri River.

"My mother had become a true Western woman and could ride, drive four horses and shoot very well," Bull related to a Cascade County, Montana newspaper decades later. "Dad and his older brothers filed on homesteads about five miles south of Sun River town and just east of Square Butte [the Cascade County butte, not the one in Chouteau County]....My dad sold out and we moved back to Sun River, where he went to work in B.A. Robertson's store. Before we left the ranch I was exposed to photography. An aunt from Glendive came to visit us when I was about 10 years old. We had a partly completed house, with a ladder fastened to the front. She took some pictures of the place. When the prints came back, the ladder was gone. That got me. I hadn't heard about retouching."

Bull's father started a store of his own in Sun River and became postmaster of the Sun River Post Office, serving from 1908 to 1944. He also built houses for farmers and managed a grain elevator. Bull started to help his father build houses the summer after his first year in high school, all the time still "wondering about that box that could do away with ladders," so he sold the *Saturday Evening Post* and other magazines to earn money to buy his first camera, from Murphy-Maclay Hardware Company in Great Falls.

"First thing I photographed was a ladder against a building, but the ladder was still there when I got the prints," said Bull. "I still hadn't heard about retouching."

One of the first photos Bull took in Great Falls was of the public library, in 1910. Bull, who had been taught by his mother on the ranch, completed grade school in Sun River and went to high school in Great Falls. "From Great Falls I went to the University of Michigan. School hours were such that I could work three hours a day for a photographer who had a camera store, dark rooms and all. By now I had found out where that ladder on the old ranch house had gone."

He continued, "First I bought a fine imported camera and then a Graflex [a fine press camera of the time]. On vacations in Sun River these cameras paid off with good action pictures, as well as financially. I had learned how to operate a motion picture camera…the summer I graduated from college I met Mrs. Frank Lloyd, wife of the top director in Hollywood. She encouraged me to go to California and the movies. My dad took a dim view of the idea but my mother was on my side, so I left for movieland."

Bull started out as first cameraman under the director of photography. After a merger formed Metro-Goldwyn-Mayer, he was given the choice of being laid off or running the still photo department and making portraits. He accepted the job and operated the department for MGM for more than thirty years. (One of Bull's contemporaries, Bert Glennon, was a Montanan by birth, who would become a director of photography in 1916 and one of the industry's most respected craftsmen, working often for such directors as John Ford and Cecil B. DeMille. The few films Glennon directed from 1928 to 1932 weren't well received, and he soon resumed his distinguished cinematography career, which he continued until his retirement in 1963.)

"All of my awards I received meant little compared to my dad's words in 1956," later said Bull. "He told me, 'I'm damn proud of you.'"

EDWARD BURNS

Born September 21, 1879, Montana
Died July 4, 1954, Los Angeles, California

Another near-complete mystery to film historians, Edward Burns acted in dozens of films in the early 1900s, including *Nemesis and the Candy Man* and *Headin' South* (both 1918) and *By Indian Post* (1919), as well as *40-Horse Hawkins* and the German film *Garragan* (1924). He died on July 4, 1954, in Los Angeles, California. He first appeared on screen as an uncredited Klansman in 1915's *Birth of a Nation* and played the roles of barfly, cowhand, townsman, stable owner, rancher, freighter, Indian, guerrilla, stable owner, stage driver and jury foreman in productions through 1944. He was the brother of actors Bob and Fred Burns.

FREDERICK DANA "FRED" BURNS

Born April 24, 1878, Fort Keogh, Montana
Died July 18, 1955, Los Angeles, California

Frederick Dana Burns was born on April 24, 1878, in Fort Keogh, Montana, a frontier territory town constructed soon after the Battle of the Little Bighorn. Fred was reputedly "an expert roper, doing multiple horse catches, fancy spinning," and for six years, he was in charge of Buffalo Bill Cody's ranch near Cheyenne, Wyoming, where he "broke" wild mustangs for Buffalo Bill's Wild West Show. His adroitness as part of the Buffalo Bill Wild West Show earned him billing as the "King of the Rope." He traveled extensively with Buffalo Bill's Wild West Show and later with the Miller brothers' 101 Ranch Wild West Show.

By 1912, he had moved to Hollywood to work in movies full time (he was joined by his brothers Edward and Bob, who also enjoyed long successful careers as actors). He appeared in twenty-three movies between 1921 and 1930 and ninety-one movies during the sound era. His first film credit comes from the 1912 short *A Girl of the West*.

He appeared in more than 265 films—mainly in westerns in small parts such as a miner, cowhand, squatter or townsman—before his death in 1955.

He can be seen in three silent films on tape today: *The Birth of a Nation* (1915), *Cyclone Jones* (1923) and *Rio Rita* (1929).

Burns died on July 18, 1955, at age seventy-seven.

Robert Emmet "Bob" Burns

Born November 21, 1884, Glendive, Montana
Died March 14, 1957, Los Angeles, California

Born in Glendive in 1884, Bob Burns was educated in Helena and later found work in Hollywood, where he starred in early Biograph one- and two-reelers and early westerns, and then he turned to character supporting roles. Burns's one-sentence biography in an old film magazine refers to him "as a Wild West performer who entered films with the Biograph Company in 1912."

For someone who had a long career in silent serials and westerns, information is surprisingly scant. According to *A Biographical Dictionary of Silent Film Western Actors and Actresses*, "He can be seen in two silent Westerns today. Nothing on his serials could be found."

His first credit is *The Spirit of the Range* (one-reel), with Mary Charleston and Fred Burns. Bob Burns appeared in at least seven westerns in 1927–28 as a supporting player, usually the sheriff. He appeared in sixty-three sound westerns.

In perhaps his most notable role, Burns, a handsome and slender six feet and 170 pounds, appeared as Sheriff Parker in *Sagebrush Trail* (1933). Wrongly imprisoned for murder, John Brant (John Wayne) decides that his best option is to escape from jail and clear his name by finding the true killer. He ends up on the lam from Sheriff Parker and attracts the attention of outlaw Bob Jones (played by Montana's Lane Chandler), who offers to let Brant into his gang.

Bob is the brother of early film stars Fred and Ed Burns.

GEORGE BURTON

Born September 17, 1898, Butte, Montana
Died December 8, 1955, Los Angeles, California

George Burton was born on September 17, 1898, in Butte. He is known for his second private role in *Shell Socked* (1926), the dentist in *Crown Me* (1928) and as a henchman in *In Old Santa Fe* (1934). In the 1920s and '30s, he appeared in many shorts, primarily in the roles of henchman, crook, laborer, ticket taker, or plotter. In his final role in the 1948 film *The Calendar*, he landed a small role as a bookie.

In the 1920s, Butte-born George Burton appeared in many shorts, primarily in the roles of henchman, crook or plotter. *Courtesy Butte Archives.*

CATHERINE SHEEHAN CARD AKA KATHRYN CARD

Born October 4, 1892, Havre, Montana
Died March 1, 1964, Costa Mesa, California

Butte-born character actress Catherine Sheehan Card is best known for her work on *Undercurrent* (1946), *Born to Kill* (1947) and *The Unsinkable Molly Brown* (1964) and for playing Mrs. MacGillicuddy, Lucy's mother, in the *I Love Lucy* series. Card's pedigree is a matter of great conjecture, with most websites and databases regurgitating Butte as her birthplace; however, a distant relative from Ireland confirmed that Card was born Catherine Sheehan in Havre, Montana, and she had a brother named George and sisters named Mary and Anna.

Her parents were Michael Sheehan and Esther McCurdy, who married in Utica, New York, on June 20, 1887. According to the relative, "We are sketchy on what happened after Michael died in Montana and the mother and two daughters went to Seattle. Esther died in Seattle on May 21, 1923."

In 1920, there is a Catherine Card living in Seattle. She was twenty-seven, divorced and living with her sister Anna; her daughter, Ada; and her mother, Esther M. Sheehan, sixty-two. Under the stage name Kathryn Card, she got her start with radio roles in the late 1930s, notably in *Uncle Walter's Doghouse*, broadcast on NBC from 1939 to 1942. According to the November 20, 1954 *Waco News Tribune*, Card was "featured in some 1,800 radio programs, most of them emanating from Chicago."

On February 8, 1954, Card made her first television appearance in an episode of *I Love Lucy*. The installment, entitled "Fan Magazine Interview," featured Card playing a slatternly woman named Minnie Finch. One newspaper noted that Card "hailed from Butte" and that Ball spent a portion of her childhood in Montana too. The following year, in the 110th episode, she was cast as a totally different character, Mrs. MacGillicuddy, Lucy's scatterbrained mother. She portrayed that character in five episodes during the 1954–55 season, appeared in three more installments during the 1955–56 season and reprised that role for the last time in one episode of *The Lucille Ball–Desi Arnaz Show*, in 1959.

LANE CHANDLER, ROBERT CHANDLER OAKES

Born June 4, 1899, North Dakota
Died September 14, 1972, Los Angeles, California

Robert Chandler Oakes was born in North Dakota, where his mother homesteaded and his father worked as a horse rancher. Census paperwork confirms that he was born in North Dakota and then resided in South Dakota and Wisconsin before Montana. According to Montana newspapers of 1926 and 1927, Chandler was reared on ranches in eastern Montana near Bainville, fifteen miles west of Williston. (Bainville is slightly west of Culbertson.)

The family eventually relocated to Helena when he was a youngster, and he graduated from high school there. His World War I draft registration card on file at the Montana Historical Society and dated September 12, 1918, lists his permanent address as the YMCA of Helena and his occupation as truck driver at the Lindsay-Helena Company warehouse in Helena. He attended Montana Wesleyan University, which later became Intermountain Union College and was destroyed in the great earthquake of 1935, and according to one source, he was the guard and tackle on its football team, which won the state collegiate championship in 1921. It has been written that he quit college to drive a summer/fall tour bus with his friend Gary Cooper at Yellowstone National Park. Chandler later recalled that he was "a passenger agent for the Yellowstone Park Transportation Co. stationed at the Old Faithful Inn."

It's often been speculated that if Gary Cooper hadn't been such an overwhelming sensation, his buddy Lane Chandler would have been the "major male star at Paramount Studios." Chandler, who followed Cooper to Hollywood from Montana, however, was no doubt a star in his own right. *Courtesy author's collection.*

29

Cooper and Chandler formed their friendship in Helena. It's often been speculated that if Cooper hadn't been such an overwhelming sensation, Chandler would have been the "major male star at Paramount Studios." At one point, according to a film biography book, "it was a toss-up at Paramount who would get the leading man role. While Cooper possessed that indefinable charisma which propelled him to superstardom, Chandler was no doubt a star in his own right."

A 1930 media press kit offered this irresistible nugget: "Lane Chandler—studio report is that the family name is Oakes—is another of those upstanding Montanans, who is adding luster to Montana's film fame. He came from the Culbertson country—about 30 miles from Culbertson, says studio statement."

Cooper went to Hollywood in 1924 and signed a contract with Metro-Goldwyn-Mayer, and Chandler later joined his pal, according to one clipping. He arrived in Hollywood on December 1, 1926. While working as an auto mechanic, he was signed as a contract player by Paramount. He appeared in a number of unbilled westerns as a bit player until 1927, when he was given his one and only lead in a silent western, *Open Range*, with Betty Bronson. After that, Chandler, red-haired and at six feet, two inches, was bumped up to leading man roles in romantic or comedy vehicles.

In 1928, Paramount cast him in a pair of solid supporting roles in *Legion of the Condemned* and *The First Kiss*, both of which starred Cooper, whom Chandler would frequently work with throughout the next few years.

The First Kiss was filmed on location in Chesapeake Bay. According to *Gary Cooper, American Hero*, the cast had an entire Pullman car to themselves, and the director gave the porter a whole dollar to look after Cooper and Fay Wray. (Cooper made four movies with Wray, the heroine of *King Kong*, including *The Legion of the Condemned* and *The First Kiss*.)

"His old Montana buddy Lane Chandler had a small part in the picture," continued author Jeffrey Meyers. "When they stopped in Kansas City, the two men went to look at the town, missed the train and had to fly to the next stop to catch up with the group."

In 1929, Chandler appeared in his first sound film, *The Studio Murder Mystery*, with Fredric March and Doris Hill. According to the Western Film Archives, "Paramount now realized that with Cooper, Richard Arlen, March, and Neil Hamilton, it had too many leading men on the roster, and during an economy move, Chandler was dropped."

He made one film at MGM with Greta Garbo, *The Single Standard*, before landing the lead in an early "Big 4" western, *Firebrand Jordan*, Chandler's first western of the sound era.

In the 1930s, he played parts in several serials, such as in Republic's *The Lone Ranger*, as well as a number of independent full-length productions and B westerns, where his roles ranged from detective in a crime drama to the supporting role of the handsome cowboy or a Texas Ranger matched up against crooks wielding Tommy guns. After that, Chandler began his long career in countless reinforcement roles, such as the army officer, doctor, rustler, rancher, the saddle pal, the leading man's buddy or the town marshal. Among his finest was a high billing in John Wayne's *Winds of the Wasteland* (1936).

Chandler survived the transition from silent to sound and successfully adapted to television, appearing in numerous TV westerns from *Rawhide* to *The Lone Ranger* throughout the '50s and '60s. The variety of roles and number of pictures Chandler played in is staggering. One film reference guide has Chandler "identified in over 300 sound era films, and this includes 130 westerns and 35 serials." His last big-screen appearance occurred in 1971 with release of *One More Train to Rob*, starring George Peppard.

On September 12, 1972, Lane Chandler died in Los Angeles at the age of seventy-three. His obituary noted that "Robert C. Oakes, formerly of Helena," suffered a heart attack in his Hollywood home.

Chief Many Treaties

Born April 11, 1874, Montana
Died February 29, 1948, Los Angeles, California

Chief Many Treaties was born on April 11, 1874, in Montana as William Malcolm Hazlett. He was an actor, known for *Go West, Young Lady* (1941), *The Law Rides Again* (1943) and *Buffalo Bill Rides Again* (1947). He appeared as "Indian," "Indian Chief" or "Iroquois Chief" in about thirty-nine credits between 1931 and 1948.

In an article written in 1934 distributed via the Associated Press, Chief Many Treaties was quoted several times in a piece titled "Indians of the

West Dusted Off Their War Bonnets Today in Moves Against Several of the White Man's Institutions and Ideas."

The article went on to describe how in Hollywood Chief Many Treaties, a six-foot Blackfoot Indian from Montana, "stalked out on the verbal warpath" with a denunciation of film directors who allegedly cast members of other races as American Indians. Jim Thorpe, world-famous athlete, joined Chief Many Treaties in denouncing the alleged impersonation "of the Indians by other races on filmland."

"This business of motion picture companies casting Mexicans, Hawaiians, Arab, Negroes and Chinese as American Indians in their productions has got to stop," Chief Many Treaties said. "It's getting so the 500 real Indians of the film city can't get a job in Hollywood anymore."

Motion picture producers said they used other races in preference to Indians because "the average redskin does not look like the Indian the motion picture public expects to see." The film audience "likes his Indian tall, husky, and well-proportioned," one director explained.

Lobby card from *The Law Rides Again* (Monogram, 1943). Chief Many Treaties, *far right*, appeared in the film as "Chief Barking Fox." Hazlett was a member of the Blackfeet tribe and a graduate of Carlisle University. *Courtesy Western Silent Era Film Association.*

Montana-born Chief Many Treaties appeared as "Indian" or "Indian Chief" or "Iroquois Chief" in about thirty-nine credits between 1931 and 1948. *Courtesy Western Silent Era Film Association.*

Nonetheless, Chief Many Treaties appears to have held some clout in his day, as this clipping from 1947 attests: "Big, broad, open-collared Chief Many Treaties is on the Screen Extras Guild board of directors to speak for all movie Indians."

He died on February 29, 1948, in Los Angeles, California.

HELEN CHRISTIAN

Born July 25, 1910, Helena, Montana

The daughter of a socially prominent politician from Helena, Helen Fitzgerald-Collins was born in the "Queen of the Mountains" in 1910. Her father, Ted E. Collins, was a member of the Montana Club, and both he and his wife were "of the number of the best-known and most popular of Helena's social circle," according to one contemporary reference.

Under the stage name Helen Christian, she received top billing in the 1937 film *Zorro Rides Again*, a twelve-chapter Republic Pictures film serial. Filmed on a budget of approximately $98,000, it was the eighth of the sixty-six Republic serials, the third with a western theme and the last produced in 1937. She had a smaller role in the 1939 film *Back Door to Heaven*. According to one film magazine, Christian deserted show business "in favor of marrying Robert Bishop, a Pennsylvania newspaper magnate and aide to Illinois Governor Henry Horner." The nuptials took place in May 1939 while the bride was appearing on Broadway in *I Must Love Someone*.

KEI THIN CHUNG

Born November 21, 1924, Montana
Died May 28, 1997, Los Angeles, California

Kei Thin Chung is a source of endless mystery, beginning with precisely where in Montana he was born, a fact lost to history. He ended up in Hollywood for certain and acted in several television shows and movies, including *The House on Telegraph Hill* as Kei, the houseboy (1951); the intern in *Love Is a Many-Splendored Thing* (1955); and a Korean lieutenant in *War Is Hell* (1961). His career spanned from at least 1947 to 1963, with his final credit as the Chinese guard in *The Three Stooges Go Around the World in a Daze*. He died on May 28, 1997, in Los Angeles.

DOROTHY COBURN

Born June 8, 1905, Great Falls, Montana
Died May 15, 1978, Los Angeles, California

Film Comment magazine lavishly introduced actress Dorothy Coburn, who appeared in a number of early Laurel and Hardy silent movies: "Dorothy Coburn is a native of Great Falls and the family home was at Helena when it wasn't up around Malta, where the Coburn ranch spread out larger than many a European principality and the Coburn name was a kind of patent of nobility. This beautiful and talented young Montanan is making rapid progress as one of the younger personalities."

Dorothy's father, Wallace Coburn, was a western poet, movie star and film director of note, and she was a niece of author Walt Coburn and granddaughter of Robert Coburn Sr., founder of the Circle C Ranch in Montana. Born to Wallace and Ann Reifenrath Coburn in Great Falls, Montana, Dorothy was raised in Prescott, Arizona.

Dorothy Coburn's most notable pairing was with Stan Laurel and Oliver Hardy, sharing screen time with the famous duo in such films as *The Second 100 Years* (1927). *Courtesy John W. Heap.*

Dorothy Coburn's documented film repertoire is extensive, including scores of films in which she acted as horse-riding stuntwoman opposite such stars as Montana's Gary Cooper. *Courtesy John W. Heap.*

Her documented film repertoire is extensive, including scores of films in which she acted as a horse-riding stuntwoman opposite such stars as Montana's Gary Cooper and Joel McCrea, as well as a stand-in for Ginger Rogers in several of her dancing films with Fred Astaire. Brunette and shapely, Coburn appeared in sixteen silent comedy shorts for *Our Gang* and Laurel and Hardy producer Hal Roach, often as the quintessential flapper, society lady, nurse or the "woman with three husbands."

Her most notable pairing was with Stan Laurel and Oliver Hardy, sharing screen time with the famous duo in such films as *The Second 100 Years* (1927) (Stan covers her backside with white paint); *Putting Pants on Philip* (1927) (she is chased around town by an overly amorous, kilt-wearing Stan); and as a dentist's nurse in *Leave 'Em Laughing* (1928).

Dorothy's characters accepted every indignity inflicted on them in cheerful stride, whether it was falling into a pit of whitewash in *The Finishing Touch* (1928), being pied in the face in *The Battle of the Century* (1927) or soaked in mud in *Should Married Men Go Home?* (1928).

After the advent of sound, she was sometimes employed as a stand-in or uncredited stuntwoman for Ginger Rogers at RKO Pictures.

After leaving the movie business in 1936, she found employment as a receptionist for an insurance company. She was married twice and died in 1978, aged seventy-two, from emphysema.

WALLACE COBURN

Born May 31, 1872, Montana
Died March 15, 1954, Los Angeles, California

"Wallace D. Coburn, the original shoot-'em-up, watch-my-smoke, whoopee-ky-otee cowpuncher and movie star, is in town." That was how the *Honolulu Star-Bulletin* trumpeted the May 1917 arrival of northern Montana's original cowboy poet and movie star in the islands.

Famous as a writer, rancher, daredevil, bronco fighter, traveler and entertainer, Wallace had gone to Hawaii to publicize his latest film, *The Sunset Princess*, produced in Los Angeles. Wallace was accompanied by his son, Robert, sixteen, and daughter Dorothy, twelve, "also well known screen performers in western plays," according to the Hawaiian newspaper.

His appearance "caused quite a sensation," according to the *Bear Paw Mountaineer*, a newspaper in Big Sandy, Montana, that kept tabs on Coburn, his wife and "their two bright-eyed children." Indeed, the Coburn name was a type of patent of nobility.

Wallace Coburn (*right*) was famous as a writer, rancher, daredevil, bronco fighter, traveler and entertainer. On the left is his friend Charles Marion Russell, the noted painter. *Courtesy John W. Heap.*

Some Montana products were famous in their time yet are almost forgotten today, such as Wallace Coburn (1872–1954), northern Montana's original cowboy poet and movie star. *Courtesy John W. Heap.*

In the mid-1910s, Wallace Coburn opened the Bison Motion Picture Show at Malta. Its walls were covered with many Indian relics and trophies, for Coburn from time to time was the grateful recipient of many rare and costly relics as an appreciation of "his kindness and sympathetic judgment toward the different tribes." *Courtesy John W. Heap.*

"The whole Coburn family are as essentially western and still as truly refined and as educated as he—which is the best," ran the story in the *Mountaineer*. "Mrs. Coburn knew the west when it was endless, unfenced stretches, just as well as her nervy mate; she has instilled in the two fine looking children the same spirit and all together they are striving for love of the west."

Wallace David Coburn was born on May 31, 1872, in northeastern Montana, among one of the last and widest mixed-grass prairie landscapes in North America. His father, Robert Coburn Sr., founded the Coburn Circle C Ranch in 1886, raising Wallace on one of the three "big spreads" that owned or controlled most of the range in southern Philips County. One account said the Coburn ranch "spread out larger than many a European principality."

Coburn maintained a fine friendship with an equally romantic character, artist Charles Marion Russell. Russell and Coburn co-wrote the 1903 book *Rhymes from a Round-up Camp*, a cheery, lively, nostalgic collection of jingles and odes of the Wild West that sold by thousands. In addition to his coauthorship, Russell illustrated the collection.

An issue of *Western American* magazine published in the 1940s featured a photo of the pair, and it quoted Charles Russell as saying, "Wallace D. Coburn is a blue-eyed, stalwart, laughter-loving lad with a face like a Galway Blazer and a smile that is worth going miles to see. Horseman of the plains, mighty hunter, ranchman, cowpuncher, scholar, wit and poet, he rounds out his career as a Westerner by being the only White Chief of the Assiniboine-Sioux, his tribal name being Peta-kooa-honga, which means Cowboy Chief."

Coburn is said to have gone into the movie business for two reasons, first because, similar to roping horses, it was exciting, and also because he wanted to perpetuate and preserve the proceedings and clothing and deportment of the West for generations to come.

In the mid-1910s, Wallace opened the Bison Motion Picture Show at Malta. Co-owned with his wife, Ann Reifenrath Coburn, its walls were covered with many Indian relics and trophies, for Coburn from time to time was the grateful recipient of many rare and costly artifacts as an appreciation of "his kindness and sympathetic judgment toward the different tribes."

In 1916, the *Anaconda Standard* described the Malta theater as "unique in that it is the only motion picture house in the United States whose walls, entrances and lobbies are adorned with Indian replicas and trophies of the hunt of such antiquity and rarity."

According to the June 24, 1916 issue of the same paper, Coburn amassed one of the country's largest collection of Indian artifacts, including war bonnets, war whistles, war clubs, war shields, tomahawks and lances "used by Indian chiefs just spoiling for a fight," as well as "a buffalo skin pouch carried by an Indian in the Lewis and Clark Expedition in 1805." Sacajawea, the noted scout, "may have fashioned it with her own hands."

In the mid-1910s, Coburn formed the Great West Film Company at Zortman, as well as a studio in St. Paul, Minnesota. "Primarily, the object of this company is to depict western life from real live scenes in a genuine western atmosphere," read one contemporary film publication of Coburn's endeavor.

"At the present time many of the film companies throw western pictures on the screen containing 'mail-order cowboys' and scenes lacking in local color and vividness and if the film company accomplishes what it has planned, it will, to an appreciable extent, revolutionize existing opinion in the minds of people who heretofore have been unable to obtain information about the West and westerners, first hand."

Equally skillful with his pen, he wrote the scenario and took the leading role in the Great West Film Company's first production, *Yellowstone Pete's Daughter*. Filmed at the Walter Coburn ranch (Walter, Wallace's half-brother, lived from 1889 to 1971 and had a successful career as a western writer) near the Little Rockies in 1916, the film made use of twenty-two artists and forty-five workmen.

The camp was outfitted with horses and packstrings, and the movie party stayed at the Great Northern Hotel in Malta. While most of the film was shot at the Coburn ranch, a few of the scenes were shot in Malta. The name "Malta" was taken off the railroad station and replaced with "Butte." John Shady's livery barn was the background for the departing stagecoach. One episode showed one thousand head of steers stampeded.

After filming, the name of the picture was changed to *The Golden Goddess*, and it was shown at the Bison Theatre. The Great West Film Company produced films for at least a few more years.

Somewhere along the line, Wallace permanently transitioned to California, where he appeared in a number of the early silent movies, including *The Bull's Eye*, released in 1917, and *The Kaiser, the Beast of Berlin* (1918).

The *Minneapolis Star* review of *The Sunset Princess* heralded Coburn for his realism as the leading man in the 1918 Great West Film Company production, "a thrilling drama of the old west....Knowing that the day of the cowboy was done but wishing that it might live on forever in the eyes of centuries, Coburn has thrown his whole soul and ability into an accurate and interesting reproduction of the real life as he knew it and in this laudable effort he has been eminently successful."

For several years, Coburn returned to the Circle C Ranch and other parts of Montana each summer; a Montana reporter from *The Fallonite* once provided this enjoyable dispatch straight from the terrain that Wallace knew intimately:

> *When Coburn is on his ranch in Montana, he can't make his feet or hands behave. Either he must be climbing up into the middle of a sun-fishin' pinto to place his life and limbs in the hands of fate or else his index finger is itching on the trigger of his .30-30 up in the wilds on the trail of a grizzly. It is this indomitable defiance of conventionality that has won him a high niche in the movie game, and thrills and diversities of which have partially taken the place of the daring day of old before barbed wire from Chicago and dry-land farmers from Iowa and elsewhere chased the cowman after the red men—into the discard.*

The Circle C Ranch was eventually sold off and became part of the Matador holdings that stretched from Texas to Saskatchewan. (The Nature Conservancy struck a "complicated" deal to preserve the sixty-thousand-acre Matador Ranch in 2000.)

Wallace lived out the remainder of his life in California, at one point operating a western museum in Hollywood. Some of the stories from his most enduring work, *Rhymes from a Round-up Camp*, were dramatized for the screen. He died on March 15, 1954, in Los Angeles.

Perhaps this quote about Wallace from an entertainment pamphlet in 1918 would be a fitting, respectful epitaph: "He is one of the few men who actually know the life and can depict it properly in verse and on the screen." His daughter, Dorothy Coburn, also became a noted film actress, appearing in a chain of Hal Roach–directed shorts and early Laurel and Hardy silent films. Dorothy died on May 15, 1978, in Los Angeles.

GARY COOPER

Born May 7, 1901, Helena, Montana
Died May 13, 1961, Beverly Hills, California

Gary Cooper was one of Hollywood's exceptional actors in leading-man roles for three decades. During his career, he came to epitomize the strong, silent type of action. Lean, handsome and shy, and characterized by a halting, hesitant delivery, he represented a brand of American integrity.

Gary Cooper, seen here in 1936, was one of Hollywood's outstanding actors in leading-man roles for three decades. *Courtesy Montana Historical Society.*

In 1885, Charles Cooper settled in Helena, which became the state capital in 1894. During the 1890s boom, Helena had fifty millionaires—more per capita than any other city in America. Charles met Alice Louise Brazier, who had also come from England to Montana to visit her brother, in 1893. Gary was born during an electrical storm on the second floor of a modest two-story red brick house, surrounded by high cottonwood trees, at 730 Eleventh Avenue. Gary went to Central grade school and Johnson grammar school.

As Charles's law career prospered (he later became a Montana state Supreme Court justice), the family moved off a main thoroughfare to three other houses, near one another and in a better part of town: a large three-story, stucco, turreted duplex at the corner of Fifth and Beattie; a shuttered two-story, wood-frame house, with a railed front porch, up a steep hill at 15 Shiland; and a brick dwelling, with a big front window and arched entrance leading to the front porch, across the street at 712 Fifth Avenue. According to one biographer, "Dressed like Huckleberry Finn, he wore a denim shirt overalls and high shoes. In those days, after the spring flood in Last Chance Gulch, he could still find enough gold flakes to buy a week's supply of licorice and candy."

Most of Gary's childhood adventures occurred on the ranch, the 7 Bar 9, which Charles bought in 1906 when Gary was five and brother Arthur was eleven. The ranch was paradise for the Cooper boys, but their genteel mother never really liked Montana. "Alice heard them swearing, was shocked by their coarse manners and thought they were turning into little savages—one step removed from the Indians." Alice had Gary and Arthur sent to England for three years. After his return to Helena, Gary hoped to become a commercial artist. He admired the western artist Frederic Remington and Charles M. Russell, a friend of Charles Cooper. Russell first came to Helena as a cowboy in 1880 and lived there until the 1890s. Cooper continued to draw and paint (frequently on the film set) throughout his life. His high school notebook contains an ink sketch of an eagle on a rock, and his daughter owns two drawings, "signed Frank Cooper" (his birth name), of an Indian head and a mountain lion. One of his political cartoons was in the *Helena Independent* on November 2, 1924.

After losing a year on his return from England and two years while working on the ranch, Gary was now three years behind his age group in school. In the spring of 1919, while attending high school in Helena, he took art courses at Montana Wesleyan University, which had been founded by the Methodists in 1890 and had moved from the Prickly Pear Valley to Helena in 1898. In the spring 1919 issue of the student magazine, the *Prickly Pear*, under the heading "Too Late to Classify," a photo of Frank Cooper appeared with the caption, "An artist of no small ability." In Helena High School, "where he had trouble readjusting to the classroom and little interest in academic subjects, he was older than most students but became notorious of pulling childish pranks and getting into mischief."

Gary didn't seem to apply himself very hard, and he was shipped off to Bozeman in 1919 to complete his last three years of high school. He attended several colleges before graduating from Grinnell College in Iowa. After graduation, he served as a guide in Yellowstone National Park. While still in Montana, he illustrated political cartoons for a Helena newspaper.

In 1924, Cooper moved to Los Angeles, where he hoped to continue with his career in cartooning. However, he began to find work in films as an extra because of his ability to ride a horse. His big break came in 1926, when he was cast as a last-minute replacement for the second lead in the successful silent film *The Winning of Barbara Worth*. While Gary adjusted well to his new life, Myrna Loy, who'd known the Coopers in Helena, felt that Alice "transplanted the poor judge from Montana to Hollywood, where he always seemed lost and lonely."

For the next three decades, Cooper starred in many memorable films under larger-than-life directors such as Frank Capra, Ernst Lubitsch, Howard Hanks and Anthony Mann. His most celebrated films include *Morocco* (1933), *Lives of a Bengal Lancer* (1935), *Mr. Deeds Goes to Town* (1936), *Meet John Doe* (1941), *Pride of the Yankees* (1942) and *Man of the West* (1958).

On February 26, 1942, Cooper won his first Oscar for his role as World War I hero Alvin York in the Howard Hawks film *Sergeant York*. On March 19, 1953, Cooper won his second Oscar for Best Actor for his enduring performance as Will Kane, the marshal who faces the outlaws alone, in the western classic *High Noon* directed by Fred Zinnemann.

The Real West, an NBC television documentary, aired on March 29, 1961, during prime time, with Cooper providing narration. The documentary was designed to clarify some of the venerable myths about America's Old West. Cooper, visibly ill from the effects of lung cancer, made his last appearance before a camera when a portion of his narration was photographed at the ghost town of Elkhorn near Helena. The American public would learn of Cooper's illness a month later when fellow actor Jimmy Stewart tearfully accepted a special Oscar for Cooper at the Academy Awards.

Cooper passed away on May 13, 1961.

WALTER COY

Born January 31, 1909, Great Falls, Montana
Died December 11, 1974, Los Angeles, California

Born in Great Falls in 1909, Walter Darwin Coy was best known for narrating the NBC western anthology series *Frontier*, which aired early Sunday evenings in the 1955–56 season.

Great Falls native Walter Coy appeared in about 141 movies and television shows, with the first in 1936 and the final in 1974, the year of his death. *Courtesy Western Film Association of America.*

Coy's parents, Theodore Coy and Luella Clapper, married in Great Falls on February 21, 1902. Coy was from Michigan, and Clapper was born in Elmira, New York.

By 1910, the family were living in Great Falls on First Avenue South and had four children, with Walter the youngest. Theodore worked as a salesman during this period. The Coy family shows up on the Great Falls city directories from 1910 to 1925, with Theodore consistently working in furniture sales. In 1915–18, Theodore owned his own furniture store, Generation Furniture.

In the 1920 census, Walter was twelve years old, and the family still resided in Great Falls, with Dad being listed as furniture merchant. The Great Falls 1925–26 city directory reported the family as "moved to Seattle, WA."

By 1928, Walter was attending University of Washington. The 1928 yearbook lists him as playing the "Duke Vivaldi" in the production of *Clari/ Maid of Milan.* The 1930 census recorded Walter and his wife, Esther, living in Manhattan, New York, where he is an actor "in theater."

According to *Shooting Stars of the Small Screen: Encyclopedia of TV Western Actors, 1946 to Present,* "Had Walter Coy become a salesman, he could have talked anyone into buying anything with a self-assured but never abrasive voice."

Coy's IMDb page lists 141 credits, with the first in 1936 and the final in 1974, the year of his death. Coy owns a piece of radio history as the first actor to play the "Lone Wolf." But it's *Frontier* that delivered him the most attention. Coy opened each *Frontier* episode with the line, "This is the way it happened...movin' west," and he closed with the refrain, "That's the way it happened...movin' west." Of the thirty-one *Frontier* episodes, sixteen are narrated by Coy.

Coy appeared in Jim Davis's western anthology series *Stories of the Century* in the role of Sam Clayton in the 1954 episode entitled "Tom Horn," an account of the western lawman turned desperado of the same name. He appeared on dozens of other western television programs, including *The Lone Ranger, Bonanza, Rawhide, The Outcasts* and *Wagon Train*.

Coy appeared as John Wayne's ill-fated older brother Aaron Edwards in the early sequences of *The Searchers* (1956), and in 1957, Coy portrayed Dr. Joseph Warren in the Walt Disney film *Johnny Tremain*, based on the 1943 historical novel of the American Revolution.

Coy's other film appearances included *The Lusty Men* (1952), *Gunmen from Laredo*, *The Gunfight at Dodge City*, Alfred Hitchcock's classic suspense film *North by Northwest* (all 1959) and as Ike Garvey in *Five Guns to Tombstone* (1960).

CROMWELL DIXON

Born July 9, 1892, Columbus, Ohio
Died October 2, 1911, Spokane, Washington

Cromwell Dixon was a true child prodigy. As a boy, he built his own roller coaster and charged the neighborhood children a penny per ride. At age eleven, fascinated with flying, he constructed two motor-driven bicycles. His first invention came to him when he was just fourteen years old: a "sky bicycle" powered by pedals and a propeller and steered with a rudder connected to the handlebars. After experimenting with the "sky bicycle," Dixon became an exhibition pilot. At nineteen, he was the youngest licensed aviator in the country—perhaps even the world.

A confident Dixon pushed the limits of his flying machine—not much more than a shabby wooden box enveloped by chicken wire—and soon he

Aviation performer Cromwell Dixon was a true child prodigy. As a boy, he built his own roller coaster and charged the neighborhood children a penny per ride. *Courtesy World Museum of Flying.*

FIRST AIRSHIP CROSSING CONTINENTAL DIVIDE
SEPT. 30-11, CROMWELL DIXON-AVIATOR,
READY FOR RETURN TO HELENA, MONT.

By guiding his fragile Curtiss bi-wing plane over the Continental Divide, Ohio-born Cromwell Dixon made history, becoming the first person to cross the Rocky Mountains by air. *Courtesy World Museum of Flying.*

perfected the "Dixon Corkscrew," an aerial exercise in which he would circle down from eight thousand feet, pull up and level off just before landing. Cromwell's celebrity even caught the attention of President William Howard Taft, who invited the entire Dixon family out to a large dinner the night before an exhibition.

"Daring Aviator Will Attempt Perilous Feat of Mountain Crossing" trumpeted the headlines in the *Helena Independent* on September 28, 1911. Curious spectators clustered at the Montana State Fairgrounds to watch Cromwell take off; others had already built a fire on the opposite side of the divide to help Cromwell identify his landing spot.

The teenager charted his famous flight over the divide, thirsting to obtain the $10,000 offered by local executives as compensation to the first aviator to traverse the Continental Divide. Throngs of people gathered to see the famous boy wonder at the Montana State Fairgrounds in Helena on September 30. One day earlier, he had enthralled much of the same audience with his daring aerial acrobatics.

He flew west of Helena and landed successfully on the west side of Mullan Pass, in a field. By guiding his fragile Curtiss bi-wing plane over the Continental Divide, the Ohio-born teenager made history, becoming the first person to cross the Rocky Mountains.

Following his successful sojourn, he flew back to the fairgrounds, where "a greater ovation than ever before given anyone at the fairgrounds was accorded Dixon when he mounted the platform," the *Helena Independent* reported. "Governor Norris publicly congratulated Dixon and declared that he was without a peer in the realm of the air. Dixon, as usual, blushed furiously, but the cries of the crowd for a speech went unanswered."

On October 2, 1911, just two days after his famous crossing, Dixon was killed when his aircraft was caught in a downdraft while performing an aerial stunt at the Spokane Interstate Fairgrounds. The biplane encountered a strong, unexpected updraft, plunging it toward the ground, crushing the nineteen-year-old pilot under the heavy engine.

Montana residents have not forgotten about this bright young inventor and brave, precocious pilot who amazed them with a stunt-flying, fast-paced life. A campground on top of MacDonald Pass, near the Continental Divide, was recently named in his honor, and a plaque at the Helena airport commemorates his flight.

CLINT DORRINGTON

Born December 25, 1898, Butte, Montana
Died June 27, 1968, Long Beach, California

Born to Frank Dorrington and Christine Thomson in Butte in 1898 as Clinton Ewan Dorrington, "Clint" secured small roles in several Hollywood productions in the 1950s, including *The Marrying Kind* (1952), *Around the World in 80 Days* (1956) and *The Last Hurrah* (1958). Between 1942 and 1958, Dorrington appeared in about a dozen films in tiny supporting roles as the railroad man, sailor, ranger, pirate or officer. He died on June 27, 1968, in Long Beach, California.

JULIAN ELTINGE

Born May 14, 1881, Newtonville, Massachusetts
Died March 7, 1941, New York City, New York

"Women went into ecstasy about him," the comedian W.C. Fields once remarked about Julian Eltinge. "Men went into the smoking room."

A long-forgotten actor, the thrill of 1900s Broadway and a gender bender of silent films, drag queen Julian Eltinge was popular in Butte, where he accepted his first theater position as an usher, along with several other lads, at the old John Maguire Opera House at Butte. During a two-day engagement in Butte at the height of his popularity, Eltinge noted that he was first bitten by the showbiz bug while he and his friends hung around the Caplice Hall (a dance hall and performance theater in Butte). "My first ambitions to mix in the theatrical game were registered then," acknowledged Eltinge.

A native of Newtonville, Massachusetts, Eltinge was born William "Bill" Julian Dalton on May 14, 1881, the only child of Michael and Julia (Baker) Dalton—so reads the date on his birth certificate, not the May 14, 1883 date he gave out during his life. He claimed that he arrived in Butte as a boy of seven, which would be 1888. That is why no Dalton listings appear in the Butte city directories for 1885–86. John Dalton begins appearing in Butte

Onetime Butte resident Julian Eltinge went on to become America's first famous female impersonator. *Courtesy Butte Archives.*

city directories starting in 1888, was listed in 1890 as a barber for E.M. Kunze and C.M. Joyce and appeared from 1893 to 1898 as a teamster and driver for Johnston and Borthwick. The entire family appears to have lived in Los Angeles and San Francisco in 1891 and 1892. Etta M. Dalton, listed in the mid-1890s as a lady clerk in Hennessy's Department Store, is most likely Julian's mother, born Julietta Baker at Lowell, Massachusetts.

Eltinge told reporters that his father had come to Butte "because of mining interests," and another time he said that the father "worked as a clerk in W.A. Clark's bank." Throughout his career, he would tell snippets of the truth to the press or wholly fabricate sagas about his childhood.

What is known to be factual is that the Dalton family periodically made its home in Butte, where the young Bill Dalton attended the old Broadway School. His best friend and classmate was a boy named Will Eltinge.

The origin of the name "Julian Eltinge" was told by R.J. Barton, Eltinge's manager. "Mr. Eltinge's real, every-day name is William Julian Dalton," Barton said. "It was through another Butte boy that his present stage designation was chosen. At school 'Billy' Dalton's best friend and chum was Will Eltinge, who later became a clerk in Clark's bank. When Billy Dalton went on the stage he took his own middle name and the last name of his chum, the result being a name quite satisfactory as theatrical title—Julian Eltinge. The other night while our show was in Spokane we had dinner with the real Will Eltinge."

When the Daltons left Butte, they headed for Boston, where they finally settled. According to several reports, a Boston dance teacher named Mrs. Wyman encouraged Eltinge to work toward becoming a female impersonator after she caught him mimicking the female students.

By 1904, Eltinge had made his first Broadway stage appearance as a female impersonator, and only two years later, Eltinge's success brought

JULIAN ELTINGE
IN
"THE FASCINATING WIDOW"

A long-forgotten actor, the toast of 1900s Broadway and a gender bender of silent films, drag queen Julian Eltinge was popular at Butte, where he accepted his first theater position as an usher. *Courtesy Butte Archives.*

him to London's Palace Theatre. Soon after, he gave a royal command performance at Windsor Castle for King Edward VII.

His first performance back in his old hometown was on January 22, 1910, when he took second billing to the Scottish comedian Harry Lauder. It was reported in the *Butte Evening News* that Eltinge, as he stepped off the train, was "met by a large delegation of personal friends." Although Lauder received the lion's share of the publicity, the *News* noted that "Eltinge, the Butte boy, in feminine characterizations, was also highly appreciated. He took his wig off when he had finished and made a little speech in which he told the size of his corsets."

Also in 1912, Eltinge returned to Butte for a three-day engagement of *The Fascinating Widow*. The *Butte Inter Mountain* praised his performance at the Broadway Theater: "Whatever your opinion in general of merry widows, there is one, the merriest widow of them all, you can't afford to miss."

The *Butte Miner* expressed this view: "Eltinge carries a dual role, unique in the history of the drama, and so difficult that it is very probable that he is the one man in the world to do it full justice."

The following year, Eltinge again played *The Fascinating Widow* in Butte. The *Butte Miner* noted that Eltinge had "lost none of his cleverness as a female impersonator and the play has lost none of its charm."

Eltinge continued to perform on the stage in such plays as *The Crinoline Girl* and *Cousin Lucy*. Additionally, Eltinge had minor roles in such silent films as *An Adventuress* in 1920, which also featured a then unknown Rudolph Valentino; *How Molly Malone Made Good* in 1915; and *Seven Chances* with Buster Keaton (1925).

Eltinge returned to Butte's Broadway Theater in 1919. During the performance, he introduced a new tune titled "The Cute Little Beaut from Butte, Montana." The show was called "a glorified vaudeville of the type that Butte theater-goers have few chances to witness...laughter was unrestrained through most of the numbers."

Eltinge continued to perform on stage and in films throughout the 1920s and early 1930s. Unfortunately, his audiences grew smaller, and his popularity dissipated. During this period of his life, he spent much of his time at his California ranch, where his mother, Julia, resided. He died in New York City on March 7, 1941.

"Julian Eltinge, as virile as anybody virile, contributed to the gaiety of nations by playing fascinating widows more fascinatingly than if fascinating real widows played them," the actress Ruth Gordon wrote in the *New York Times* on August 31, 1969.

AGNES FRANEY

Born August 31, 1891, Montana
Died December 14, 1975, Alameda, California

The mysterious Agnes Franey appeared in several films in the 1920s, including *The Singing Fool* (1928), *Stolen Kisses* (1929) and *Queen of the Night Clubs* (1929). Both Franey and Billings-born Helen Lynch appeared in the September 19, 1928 Warner Bros. release *The Singing Fool*, appearing as "balloon girl" and "maid," respectively. Franey ostensibly had a friendship with Helena-born Myrna Loy, and they appeared in a photo shoot together in 1929 captioned "Seaside flappers Agnes Franey and Myrna Loy show off the latest 1929 beach fashions." It's most likely that the pair met on the set of *Queen of the Night Clubs*, released by Warner Bros. on March 16, 1929, in which Loy received "unverified credit" in a bit role in the film directed by Bryan Foy, while Franey is listed as "flapper."

While details of Franey's connection to and life in Montana are ambiguous, an early reference in the *Montana Standard* in 1930 refers to her as a Butte girl and former "Camp Fire" kid.

Founded in 1910 by Luther Gulick, MD, and his wife, Charlotte Gulick, Camp Fire's mission was "to guide young people on their journey to self-discovery." According to the article, "Camp Fire was America's first nonsectarian and multicultural organization for girls."

TAYLOR GORDON

Born April 29, 1893, White Sulphur Springs, Montana
Died May 5, 1971, White Sulphur Springs, Montana

Emmanuel Taylor Gordon's life began between six and seven o'clock on Saturday morning, April 29, 1893, at White Sulphur Springs, Montana, in a little three-room shack with two gables, two doors, four windows and a cloth ceiling.

Taylor was the youngest of five children of John Francis Gordon Sr. and Mary Anna Goodall Gordon. His father claimed descent from Zulu ancestors, and his mother was born in slavery in Bourbon County, Kentucky.

The mysterious Agnes Franey appeared in several films in the 1920s, including *The Singing Fool* (1928). *Courtesy Butte Archives.*

The couple and their baby son, Robert, moved to Montana from Cairo, Illinois, in 1881, traveling up the Missouri River via steamboat. John worked as a cook in the gold mining camps of Barker and Castle and for cattle roundups.

Their daughter, Rose, was born in Barker in 1883. Sometime around 1885, the family moved to White Sulphur Springs, where they became—and remained—the town's only African American family.

The senior Gordon left White Sulphur Springs in 1895; he headed out for the Alaskan gold fields but reportedly was killed in a train crash in Canada. Mary raised the children alone, supporting the children primarily by working as a laundress.

Young Taylor Gordon spent his early years attending the local school and carrying out a variety of offbeat jobs, including messenger for the town's brothels, pin setter in a bowling alley and preparer of opium in the town's Chinese opium den, before he left home to become a chauffeur, Pullman porter, auto mechanic and chef in the personal train cars of circus owner John Ringling. Ringling had a ranch near White Sulphur Springs (the tiny town of Ringling bears the family name).

White Sulphur Springs was a "cultured cowtown" then. Its population was about eight hundred, but it had eight or ten grand pianos. Some of the country's best stage shows played in the old auditorium operated by Robert Sutherland, and it was a time of jovial and fancy parties. The Gordon home was filled with music; all members of the family sang and played various instruments. Mary Gordon was renowned for the haunting beauty and power of the spirituals she sang. Taking a cue from his mother, Taylor—or "Mannie" Gordon, as he was called—would sing as he worked.

In about 1910, when Taylor was seventeen, Ringling hired him as chauffeur for his Smith River Development Company and later chef and porter on his private railroad car. Taylor traveled around the United States on the train, experiencing for the first time the prejudice and hostility facing black Americans in the 1910s and 1920s.

In 1910, the St. Paul, Minnesota opera house manager Louis N. Scott, who had visited Montana as John Ringling's guest, hired Gordon as his personal chauffeur. Also working as a Pullman porter, doorman and cook, Gordon eventually made his way to New York, where he became Ringling's valet, traveling throughout the country on Ringling's private rail car. In 1915, in St. Louis, Missouri, a passerby overheard Gordon singing along to an Enrique Caruso record and suggested that he pursue a musical career. With Ringling's support, he moved to New York to study with composer Will

In New York City, Montana's Taylor Gordon became a vibrant figure in the Harlem Renaissance, the cultural, social and artistic explosion that took place in Harlem, New York, between the end of World War I and the middle of the 1930s. *Courtesy Matthew Maynard Collection.*

Marion Cook, and after stints as a dockworker, bricklayer, elevator operator and immigration agent, he began performing with B.F. Keith's vaudeville revue in 1919.

In New York City, Gordon became a vibrant figure in the Harlem Renaissance, the cultural, social and artistic explosion that took place in Harlem, New York, between the end of World War I and the middle of the 1930s. During this period, Harlem was a cultural epicenter, attracting black writers, artists, musicians, photographers, poets and scholars.

Gordon partnered with pianist Rosamond Johnson in 1925 in a musical vaudeville act, performing spirituals. The duo toured for several years, including a series of concerts in Europe in 1927, before separating in the early 1930s. As an interpreter of "Negro spirituals," he was written to have had "no equals." Gordon's career peaked in 1927 when he toured France and England, performing for a number of dignitaries, including England's King George V and Queen Mary. An article in the *Billings Gazette* in 1928 refers to Gordon as "the Negro singer who put Montana on the map."

Gordon continued entertaining privately and eventually pursued an acting career, appearing as a cast member on Broadway in *Shoot the Works* (1931), *Ol' Man Satan* (1932), *The Gay Divorcee* (1932) and *After Such Pleasure* (1934), as well as in the film *The Emperor Jones* (1933), with Paul Robeson. Yet he never reclaimed his previous level of success. In 1929, Gordon's autobiography, *Born to Be*, was published; it remains of note because of its insightful perspective on race and race relations in the West at a time when few African Americans lived there. Gordon's presentation of his childhood in Montana scarcely mentions his race and portrays a perhaps romanticized view of all kinds of people living together in a small town with little or no conflict.

Gordon returned to White Sulphur Springs in 1935 and spent the winter of that year in a cabin at Sheep Creek Ranch. It became increasingly difficult for Gordon to make a living, as his attempts to renew his musical career fell short. He eventually turned to inventing toys and working as a lathe operator in a New Jersey B-29 factory during the World War II.

Gordon suffered a mental breakdown in 1947 and was hospitalized in New York for most of the following twelve years. In February 1959, Gordon was released from Central Islip Hospital into the care of his sister, Rose, who still resided in White Sulphur Springs. He lived there in anonymity, surviving on rental incomes and an antique business. He also occasionally provided concerts and talks for local groups.

In 1960, Gordon's songs rolled out with all the warmth and feeling that had started his vocal career many years before. He sang with his fine tenor voice, reaching out over the silent auditorium, whose audience had braved subzero weather to attend the concert of a hometown artist. His winter concert was his first in Montana in almost a quarter of a century. "The people who heard it seemed quite pleased," said Gordon to the *Great Falls Tribune*, "so if I can rake up the music I want I'll be singing some more soon…and in between, I hope I'll be able to develop a few things I have in mind. If I can afford the expense I feel sure they will be enjoyed by many people."

He continued to write, including the 1970 *Born to Be* sequel, but his only other publication was a 1967 booklet entitled *The Man Who Built the Stone Castle*, describing White Sulphur Springs' historic landmark and its creator, B.R. Sherman.

Taylor Gordon died on May 5, 1971. Shortly beforehand, future novelist Ivan Doig taped his reminiscences of Harlem in the 1920s. Gordon was the inspiration of Doig's Monty Rathbun in the popular novel *Prairie Nocturne*. Rathbun is a black chauffeur whom music teacher Susan coaches, with Wes's financial backing. In the book's preface, Doig refers to Gordon as "a gifted singer who went to New York, blazed through the Harlem Renaissance and got a little famous, then blew his money and wound up back in Montana."

None of Taylor's four siblings married or had children.

Gordon's son Robert (1881–1962) lived in White Sulphur Springs, working several years as the custodian for the Sherman Hotel and the First National Bank. Rose Gordon (1883–1968) was born in Barker, Montana, and lived in White Sulphur Springs, operating various businesses (Rose's Café, Kentucky Kitchen and Gordon Novelty) and working as a physical therapist. John Gordon Jr. (1885–1952) was born in White Sulphur Springs and worked thirty years for the Dollar Steamship Line, headquartered in Seattle. George Washington Gordon (1888–1948) was born in White Sulphur Springs and served twenty-nine years as a steward for the Bozeman Elks Club.

KAY HAMMOND

Born December 14, 1901, Helena, Montana
Died January 7, 1982, Los Angeles, California

Although all the major film and movie databases list her birthplace as Kansas City, Kansas, Kay Hammond was indisputably born in Helena, Montana.

Kay Hammond is also typically confused, even in filmographies, with the sophisticated English actress Dorothy Katherine Standing (1909–1980), who adopted "Kay Hammond" as a stage name. Treasure State Kay was the granddaughter of the Judge Barrett, who for years held the office of state treasurer. She was the daughter of Mr. and Mrs. Boyd Hammond, who lived on Ewing Street until about 1918, when they moved to Los Angeles.

Hammond appeared on the legitimate stage in many successful plays, and her appearance with Gloria Swanson in the 1929 film *The Trespasser*, "a sensational drama of modern life, with the upper social strata of Chicago as its setting," was her first time in pictures. That same year, she also appeared as Julia Sturm in *Her Private Affair*. In "private life" she was Mrs. Weatherby, marrying one of the Weatherby boys of the Weatherby-Kaiser Shoe company of Los Angeles. Hammond kept many friends in Helena and a number of relatives, among them Mrs. Rudolph Horsky and Dr. Ben C. Brooke, who were cousins. In a snippet announcing the debut of *The Trespasser* at the Marlow, the *Helena Daily Independent* noted Hammond's Montana roots and that she had never appeared in any play in Helena; it added that her appearance "will afford her friends and relatives their first opportunity of seeing her since starting her career on the stage."

The *Montana Standard* also kept tabs on Kay Hammond, including this reference in 1930: "Kay Hammond, going into the pictures after a successful stage career, is the granddaughter of a well known Montana pioneer, who was a Montana state treasurer. Her parents were well known residents of Helena."

GILBERT "PEE WEE" HOLMES

Born June 15, 1895, Miles City, Montana
Died August 17, 1936, Hollywood, California

Gilbert "Pee Wee" Holmes was born in Miles City on June 15, 1895, and played sidekick to such stars as Tom Mix, Jack Hoxie, Dustin Farnum, Hoot Gibson and Fred Humes. He was also in twenty-two two-reelers with Ben Corbett. Holmes can be seen in five movies on film or tape today. According to the *Biographical Dictionary of Silent Film Western Actors and Actresses*, "'Pee Wee' was beloved and known by (I dare say) all of the kids of the 20s. It is hard to believe this is (his birth and death dates and filmography) the only information on him found in reference books today." Several tantalizing references have survived, such as this interview with the *Afton Star Valley Independent* in 1929 in advance of the film *Quick Triggers*: "Holmes remembers way back when they uster' carry the readin' in the chuck wagon. Even the night hearders would crawl up close to the fire and read till the wee small hours." A newspaper advertisement for the January 1932 opening of the Pee Wee Holmes New York School of Dancing touted specialized instruction in "Tap-Ballet-Acrobatic-Musical Comedy-Buck and Wing-Military-Waltz Clog-Tango Fox Trot Waltz," as well as stage dancing by Holmes,

Gilbert "Pee Wee" Holmes was born in Miles City on June 15, 1895, and played sidekick to such stars as Tom Mix, Jack Hoxie, Dustin Farnum, Hoot Gibson and Fred Humes. *Courtesy Western Silent Era Film Association.*

formerly head instructor in the leading New York schools and Warner Bros. and Tiffany Pictures star.

Standing five feet, three inches, Holmes, hailed as a skilled comedian, finished his film career with nine sound westerns, mostly comedies.

ESTHER HOWARD

Born April 4, 1892, Butte, Montana
Died March 8, 1965, Hollywood, Los Angeles, California

For someone who appeared in more than one hundred films in a twenty-three-year-career, details of Esther Howard's life are remarkably scant. The most common foul of Wikipedia and the regurgitating movie databases is the location of her birth. Howard's birth certificate notes that she was born on April 4, 1892, in Butte to James W. Howard Jr. and Martha Esther Boggs. At the time of her birth, the family resided at 261 East Broadway, and James was employed as a music teacher at the city's public schools. Her grandfather James W. Howard Sr. was a respected physician whose office was located at 29 West Granite. Born in California in 1842, Dr. Howard moved to Dillon in 1884 and then moved to Butte, where he remained for ten or twelve years. While in Butte, Dr. Howard served as the first secretary of the public library of that city and was one of the members of the original Silver Bow Medical Society; he also served one term as coroner of Silver Bow County.

Esther Howard is listed in the 1910 U.S. Census as living on Haviland Street with her parents and younger brother, Robert, in Boston Ward 10, Suffolk, Massachusetts. We know that Esther came from an artistic family. Her father had moved from Boston to Montana to become musical conductor of the Butte Opera House. He brought his wife, formerly Martha Boggs, a dramatic soprano who had toured the country with John Philip Sousa. When their daughter was five, the time had come to return to Boston. James W. Howard Jr.'s Masonic membership card lists his residence in Boston and dates his initiation in "Butte #22 Montana" on April 27, 1892.

Esther was sent to boarding school, where she "struggled bravely." She told the *New York Times* in 1927 that "she hated school, loathed education and everything even remotely associated with learning."

While a senior at Girls' Latin School in Boston, Esther read in the newspaper that "supers" were wanted at the Tremont Theatre for "the mob scene in Madame X," starring Sarah Bernhardt, and she "staged a fainting spell realistically enough to land her first job."

Esther entered into a stock company at Lynn, Massachusetts, and by age twenty-five, she had taken "her comic timing, expressive eyes and soprano voice far" from Montana to the stage of New York City Broadway comedies and musical revues, including featured roles in hits such as *Sunny* and *The New Moon*.

Esther left New York City for Hollywood in 1930, tallying twenty-eight credited movies and dozens of unglamorous parts to her name, including tenement dweller, streetwalker and lunch counter lady.

Although mostly support, she did earn a variety of good roles in her career, appearing in a range of roles from confused farm girl to bejeweled wife in seven of screenwriter Preston Sturges's pictures. She is perhaps best recollected for the role of Jessie Florian in Edward Dmytryk's classic noir *Murder, My Sweet*. Her last role of significant note was as the mother of Kirk Douglas and Arthur Kennedy in Mark Robson's *Champion* (1949), although she can be seen in movies throughout the 1940s and 1950s as a range of landladies, boardinghouse owners, madams and pithy-speaking bystanders.

Esther Howard passed away from a heart attack on March 8, 1965, at the age of seventy-four. Her obituary in *Film Comment* emphasized the odd mixture of roles she handled with characteristic aplomb: "Switching from Broadway to Hollywood in 1931, actress Esther Howard was an expert at portraying blowsy old crones, man-hungry spinsters and oversexed dowagers. Utilizing her wide, expressive eyes and versatile voice for both broad comedy and tense drama, Howard was equally at home portraying the slatternly toss-pot or the genteelly homicidal."

PERT KELTON

Born October 14, 1907, Simms, Montana
Died October 30, 1968, Ridgewood, New Jersey

"A 17 year old Montana girl now has her name in the big electric lights on Broadway and thousands of New Yorkers jam their way into the New York Amsterdam theater every night to see her do her stuff."

So raved the *New York Tribune* in 1924 about the young eccentric comedienne who was born near Great Falls in 1907.

The daughter of vaudeville performers Edward and Susan Kelton, Pert Kelton was born on October 14, 1907, on the Simms ranch on Box Elder Creek, one mile south of the Highwood road, east of Great Falls.

Edward and Susan obtained a string of touring vaudeville contracts when Pert was a little girl. In 1911, while accompanying her parents and sister on an overseas tour of shows, she debuted on stage at the age of three in Cape Town, South Africa. (Her aunt, Jane Kelton, was also a professional actress in the early 1900s. Jane is credited with giving the bright, vivacious Pert her name while reminiscing to Pert's mother about her career and describing her favorite theatrical role, the character "Pert Barlow" in a play called *Checkers*.)

At age six, her parents added her to their act, and the "Three Keltons" attracted the attention of eastern booking offices. By the mid-1920s, they were being sent over the larger circuits, such as Keith's and the Orpheum. She appeared with her mother as "a sister act," Pert and Sue Kelton, in which Pert played the trombone and Sue the clarinet, both danced and Pert also gave impersonations of Charlie Chaplin and William S. Hart. The act finished with the two women providing vocal imitations of the trombone and clarinet.

In 1925, Pert was given the four-minute cameo role of an eccentric comedienne in *Sunny*, Jerome Kern's 1925 Broadway musical comedy starring Marilyn Miller. Soon her name was flashing from huge electric signs and well known among Broadway theatergoers in New York, prompting the dramatic critic of the *New York Morning Telegram* to write, "And now look at her name up in lights on Forty-second! Rural papers, please don't copy; keep the farm girl on the farm. There's a thousand awful flops for every Pert on Broadway."

Her first credited movie role was as Rosie the maid in the 1929 release *Sally*, a production based on the Broadway hit by the same name. The 1930 U.S. Census reveals that Pert was residing in Los Angeles in the Warner-Kelton Hotel and sharing a room there with her parents. That same census identifies all three of the Keltons as employed actors in "motion pictures."

Pert appeared in several top films throughout the 1930s, even playing herself in the 1935 short *A Night at the Biltmore Bowl*. After her appearance in the 1939 film *Whispering Enemies*, she returned to theater and radio and then increasingly found work in television beginning in the 1950s. (Her finances must have dwindled, as in February 1940, she filed a voluntary petition of bankruptcy.)

Kelton was the original Alice Kramden in "The Honeymooners" comedy sketches on the DuMont's *Cavalcade of Stars*. These sketches formed the

Pert Kelton, una de las cómicas más atractivas de RKO-Radio, contempla al mar desde su yatecito.

While accompanying her parents and sister on an overseas tour of vaudeville shows, Pert Kelton debuted on stage at the age of three in Cape Town, South Africa. *Courtesy Great Falls Historical Society.*

Simms native Pert Kelton, whose name shined in the lights of old Broadway and who was the first actress who played Alice Kramden in the early "The Honeymooners" sketches with Jackie Gleason. *Courtesy Great Falls Historical Society.*

eventual basis for the 1955 CBS television sitcom *The Honeymooners.* On October 5, 1951, the four-minute sketch, with Kelton playing Alice, was the shaky first step toward the eventual hit show, whose thirty-nine episodes on CBS in the 1955–56 season are among the most watched comedies in television history.

The opening episode is little more than a bickering match between Ralph and Alice about dinner that turns into a competition to see who can chuck the biggest object out the window. As played by Kelton, Alice is a tough, beaten bird with some hard, dispirited miles on her.

Kelton was released from her role as a result of McCarthy-era blacklisting, replaced by Audrey Meadows. Due to her and her husband's implication as

Communist sympathizers by the scurrilous publication *Red Channels*, she was axed, and the producers falsely explained that her departure was due to "heart problems."

Age may also have had something to do with Kelton's replacement, according to some television historians. Kelton was nine years older than Gleason, while her replacement was six years younger.

In the late 1960s, Kelton was invited back to *The Honeymooners* to play Mrs. Gibson, Alice's mother, in an episode of the hour-long musical version of the popular sitcom. Kelton appeared in a number of television programs, commercials and movies (most noticeably playing the feisty Irish mother Mrs. Paroo in *The Music Man*) up until her death on October 30, 1968. Her obituary in the *New York Times* refers to her "as a character actress who specialized in gangsters' molls and hard-boiled Brooklyn gals."

HAL C. KERN

Born July 14, 1894, Anaconda, Montana
Died February 24, 1985, Los Angeles, California

Anaconda-born Hal C. Kern worked on *Gone with the Wind* and many other major motion pictures during a fifty-year Hollywood career that began in the era of silent films. Kern, who was supervising film editor for producer David O. Selznick for sixteen years, was a co-winner of an Oscar for the editing on *Gone with the Wind* in 1939 and was nominated for *Rebecca* in 1940 and *Since You Went Away* in 1944.

ETHAN LAIDLAW

Born November 25, 1899, Butte, Montana
Died May 25, 1963, Los Angeles, California

He traded gunfire with Tom Mix and Hoot Gibson. He brawled with heavy fists against the likes of Gene Autry and the Cisco Kid. Stout, bearded and menacing, Ethan Laidlaw fit the prescribed role of the baddie in westerns as well as any actor.

He worked steadily in silent and sound westerns as well as serials and TV shows for forty-plus years, in approximately 492 productions between 1923 and 1963. In them he was usually nameless—just one of a half dozen or so specialists in characterizing a scoundrel.

Born on November 25, 1899, in Butte, Montana, the son of Charles P. Laidlaw and Mary Olas, Ethan Allen Laidlaw's earliest jobs include working as a bus driver, mechanic, steam fitter, painter, policeman and salesman. When he registered for the World War I draft in 1918, he was working for the Burroughs Adding Machine Company in Butte. One newspaper reference to Laidlaw alluded to the fact that he "obtained an engineering degree" but supplied no details.

What led him to Hollywood is unknown, but his six-foot-one, 180-pound frame, strong presence and menacing looks endowed him with a hawkish aura that automatically branded Laidlaw as a villain.

His earliest traceable movie is *The Hunchback of Notre Dame* (1923), and his first credited western was *No Man's Law* (1925) with Bob Custer. All total, he appeared in more than 220 films, of which approximately 134 were westerns, and more than 20 serials.

In the beginning, he made fifty dollars per day accepting assignments for Universal Studios, often the assignment no more of a chore than sitting in a theater audience. Laidlaw scarcely spoke onscreen, often grimacing through his tiny but efficient parts as the henchman or scoundrel. His most memorable roles include *Cowboys from Texas* (1939), *Law and Order* (1940), *Fugitive from Sonora* (1943), *Marshal of Gunsmoke* (1944), *Six Gun Law* (1948) and *Trail of the Rustlers* (1950).

Laidlaw's looks enhanced western films, but his threatening mug suited gangster films and even Three Stooges, Abbott and Costello and the Ritz Brothers comedies. Laidlaw was also a thirty-year veteran of cinema sea spectacles in support of such stars Milton Sills, Errol Flynn and Alan Ladd in such films as *The Black Pirate*.

Solvent as an actor into his sixties, Laidlaw found TV work into his sixth decade on shows such as *Bat Masterson*, *Wild Bill Hickok*, *Destry* and *Wyatt Earp*.

At the time of his death at age sixty-three, from a heart attack, he was living in the Hollywood neighborhood in Los Angeles.

IRENE LENTZ

Born December 8, 1901, Brookings, South Dakota
Died November 15, 1962, Los Angeles, California

She was the fabulous Baker, Montana girl who had built "Irene" into a quality trademark. Twice Oscar-nominated for costume decoration and revered for her luxurious dresses, gowns and day skirts, Irene Lentz was one of the four graduating students to be part of the fourth class to receive diplomas at Baker High School and was involved in the entertainment at the commencement, held at the Lake Theatre on May 22, 1919. The *Baker Sentinel* noted, "While the class was small, only four graduating this year, it is one the city and school may well be proud of. The war was the cause of the small class as several boys who were Seniors tendered their services to Uncle Sam and joined the colors."

Planning to be a concert pianist, Irene traveled to California and enrolled in the music class at the University of Southern California, where she also dabbled in acting. In September 1923, the *Baker Sentinel* noted that Lentz would be supporting leading comedian Ben Turpin in a two-reel farce, *Ten Dollars or Ten Days.* "Miss Irene Lentz, a former Baker girl, is making a name for herself in the Mack Sennett Film Company and is under the direction of Del Lord appearing in a new two reel comedy," the paper reported.

In 1923, when Lake Theatre advertised *Tailor Made Man*, the ad noted that the all-star cast featured "one of our home girls, Irene Lentz, as the leading lady with Charles Ray."

She spent time in Los Angeles in 1925, working as a movie extra along with designer Walter Plunkett. Around this time, her college roommate, with ambitions to be a designer of women's clothes, planned a night course at a Los Angeles designing school but was too shy to go alone and persuaded Irene to accompanying her. After the first lesson, Irene decided she wanted to design clothes.

Shortly after completing the course, she opened a dress shop on the USC campus. Inexpensive numbers were her specialty: the top price, $29.50. Her designs caught the attention of the "Hollywood crowd." The Irene Salon opened at 9000 Sunset Boulevard, and her designs in the 1930s were hailed as "California Fresh" in the press. It was reputed to be the first boutique committed to a single designer inside a major American store.

She began dressing some of Hollywood's biggest female stars in 1933, and while credited only as "Irene," she began working for United Artists and Columbia Pictures. Irene amassed a following among the wealthy wives and family members of studio execs, including MGM chief Louis B. Mayer's daughters, Irene and Edith. Then one day in 1942, Mayer offered her the job as head of MGM's costume department, replacing the famed Adrian.

According to one magazine, the move established her reign "as the West's most sought-after designer." According to another contemporary fashion magazine, during this period Irene's "frugal Montana background proved something as a handicap." She could never look customers in the eye and tell them the elevated price, so she hired "a stooge" to follow her around on opening day and "answer the embarrassing questions about price."

In 1947, another group of about twenty-five stores, including Bergdorf Goodman and Neiman Marcus, provided half the capital for Lentz to leave MGM studio to set up her own enterprise. With the stores' financing, she made clothes exclusively for them to sell under her "Irene" brand name.

Lentz costumed Hollywood's Golden Age stars for the big screen, including scandalously clad Lana Turner in *The Postman Always Rings Twice* in 1946. She also dressed them in real life, boasting a celebrity clientele that would come to include Marilyn Monroe, Ava Gardner and Carole Lombard. Lentz was nominated for an Academy Award for Best Costume Design, Black-and-White, for *B.F.'s Daughter* (1948) and Best Costume Design, Color, for *Midnight Lace* (1960). The final film she worked on appeared in theaters in 1963.

On November 15, 1962, a few weeks before her sixty-second birthday, under an assumed name, Irene checked herself into Hollywood's Knickerbocker Hotel. She went to her room and downed two pints of vodka. She purportedly "slashed her wrists" and then leaped out an eleventh-floor bathroom window. She landed on a suspension awning, and her body was discovered later that night. A suicide note read, "I'm sorry. This is the best way. Get someone very good to design and be happy. I love you all, Irene."

She was interred at Forest Lawn Memorial Park in Glendale with first husband, F. Richard Jones. A few weeks before her death, Irene had allegedly confided in her friend, actress Doris Day, that "she had been in love with Gary Cooper" and he was "the only man she had ever loved." (Cooper had succumbed to cancer the year before.)

Although she had earned large sums of money, at the time of her death she was broke and in ill health. In a 1983 article in the *Seattle Times*, the author wrote of the designer, "Irene reads like a Greek tragedy....She had

Beginning her Hollywood career as an actress playing ingénue parts opposite Mack Sennett's leading comedians, Baker native Irene Lentz was nominated for the Academy Award for Best Costume Design, Black-and-White, for *B.F.'s Daughter* (1948) and Best Costume Design, Color, for *Midnight Lace* (1960). *Courtesy O'Fallon Historical Museum.*

an unhappy marriage, a bad drinking problem, there were rumors of a romance with Gary Cooper that fell apart, and she never felt that the fashion press appreciated her."

In the October 1937 *Cosmopolitan*, there is a two-page article on "Irene" of Hollywood, which stated that she "was born on a Fallon county homestead" and received her education in Baker. That same article also summed up, in a few words, just how large and how unusual were the achievements of Irene Lentz, the girl from Baker, Montana: "Irene, at thirty-five, is responsible for every costume in every film produced by the largest moving picture company in the world (MGM). So far as her studio is concerned, Irene has no last name. Very few people get along like that. I can think of only two who did—Topsy and Cleopatra."

MYRNA LOY

Born August 2, 1905, Helena, Montana
Died December 14, 1993, New York City, New York

Born Myrna Adele Williams on August 2, 1905, in Radersburg, in the Crow Creek Valley of Montana—forty miles southeast of Helena—Myrna Loy's father, David Franklin Williams, served in the Montana state legislature. In addition to working in banking, ranching and real estate, David was the youngest person ever elected to the Montana state legislature, at twenty-six. "That's where I got my interest in politics," said Loy to Rex Reed of the *New York Times* in 1969. "He was quite a gourmet for Montana. He used to import cracked crab on ice from Chicago."

Her mother wanted to name her Annabelle, but her father had once seen from a train window a sign with "Myrna" written on it, so she was named after a railroad whistle stop. Her grandfather was a Welsh boy who came to America and started a pony express.

At age seven, Myrna moved with her father; mother, Della Mae Johnson; and brother, David, to Helena, where they lived on Fifth Avenue, a few blocks from the Lewis and Clark County Jail. In Helena, her father became a banker, and the family lived "high off the hog on Fifth Avenue, which was not, of course, Fifth Avenue, New York," as she was once quoted. It may not have been New York, but it was just up the street from Judge Cooper and his family—including son Gary. But Gary Cooper was four years older than Myrna and often away at school. The two didn't spend much time together, until reuniting in Hollywood. And even then, she once wrote, they "curiously, seldom talked about our Helena days."

Myrna Loy's witty portrayal of Nora Charles in the *Thin Man* films of the 1930s and '40s transformed her into a screen legend. *Courtesy Montana Historical Society.*

Myrna Williams made her stage debut at age twelve at Helena's long-since demolished Marlow Theater in a dance she choreographed, based on "The Blue Bird" from the *Rose Dream* operetta. When she was thirteen, Myrna's father died of Spanish influenza before he had reached his fortieth birthday, and the rest of the family moved to Los Angeles. She was educated in L.A. at the Westlake School for Girls, where she discovered the joy of acting.

She started at the age of fifteen when she appeared in local stage productions in order to help support her family. Some of the stage plays were held in Hollywood's epic Grauman's Egyptian Theatre. Mrs. Rudolph Valentino happened to be in the audience one night, and she managed to pull some strings to secure Myrna small parts in the motion picture industry.

The name "Loy" was adopted as a professional stage name in 1925 because it sounded Oriental, and for seven years she played nothing but Chinese, Japanese, Javanese, Azuri, Spanish, Malayan and Hindu sirens, with an occasional "quadroon" thrown in for luck. Loy finally played a Caucasian with Jeanette MacDonald and Maurice Chevalier in *Love Me Tonight*, and MGM began to throw her a few sophisticated bones.

Myrna Loy's witty portrayal of Nora Charles in the *Thin Man* films of the 1930s and '40s transformed her into a screen legend. Charles stands as one of film's most treasured and timelessly entertaining characters.

Loy and William Powell appeared in fourteen films together, including six sequels to *The Thin Man*. In 1936, a poll of 20 million fans voted her "Queen of the Movies" and Clark Gable "King," and the two were subsequently paired in a number of films.

She garnered headlines with *Manhattan Melodrama* (1934) when the gangster John Dillinger—who was a fan—was killed after leaving a showing of the film in Chicago. It was primarily a medium for Clark Gable, with Loy as the woman loved by both him and Powell.

Loy achieved a popularity that exceeded that of the studio's preeminent queens. At the zenith of her fame, she and her first husband had a butler, chauffer, cook, several gardeners and live-in maids at their magnificent Hidden Valley estate, above Coldwater Canyon in Los Angeles.

Always active politically, she found herself called a Communist in 1946 by the *Hollywood Reporter*, and she sued for $1 million; she settled for a retraction and became one of the most vocal critics of the right-wing activities of Wisconsin senator Joseph McCarthy. She was one of the observers of the first meetings of the United Nations and during this period was active working for UNESCO (United Nations Educational, Scientific, and Cultural Organization).

Loy returned to Helena in October 1966 to attend graveside services at a Helena cemetery for her mother, Mrs. Della Williams, a Radersburg native and former Helena resident who died in Hollywood at eighty-six. She was buried beside her husband, David. Described as still "red-haired, pert-nosed, unpretentious and vibrantly lovely," Loy remained for a nostalgic visit with relatives and friends, which included visiting the Radersburg cattle ranch, which was one of her childhood homes, and a glimpse of the former family home on Fifth Avenue, as well as a look at St. Peter's Hospital, where she was born.

A diagnosis of breast cancer forced Myrna Loy into surgery in 1975 and again in 1979. She appeared in films until 1981.

In 1989, U.S. Senator Max Baucus met with Loy at her Upper East Side New York City apartment to ask permission to use her name for a new theater planned in Helena. To help coax her, he arrived with a box of bon bons from the Parrot in Helena. When the Myrna Loy Center for the Performing Arts celebrated its grand opening in January 1991, Loy was in failing health and unable to attend the ceremony. She was never nominated for an Oscar. However, in 1991, the Academy mitigated this oversight by giving her a special lifetime award.

On December 14, 1993, Myrna Loy passed away at Lenox Hill Hospital in New York City during surgery. By the time Myrna passed away at the age of eighty-eight, she had appeared in a staggering 129 motion pictures. She was cremated and her ashes interred at Forestvale Cemetery in Helena.

BARBARA LUDDY

Born May 25, 1908, Helena, Montana
Died April 1, 1979, Los Angeles, California

Barbara Luddy's earliest days are shrouded in mystery; most accounts have her as "a native of Helena, the family being well known," and claim that her grandfather was a pioneer and "a factor in advancing the welfare of the state." While some newspaper accounts said that she was "educated at Butte and Great Falls," others said that Barbara was born in Great Falls and spent the early days of her life "in Montana with her mother." The April 1938 edition of *Screenplay* noted that Luddy was born in Helena in 1910, nicknamed "Babs" almost at birth.

For certain, her father died while she was still a baby. At the insistence of an aunt, she nearly became a missionary but became an entertainer instead when nuns at the Ursuline Convent in Great Falls discovered that she was gifted with a voice of remarkable range and beauty. Later, she moved to

While she appeared in small parts in several well-known films, Barbara Luddy found fame and a steady paycheck in voiceover work for Disney. *Courtesy Montana Historical Society.*

Butte, and when the world war came, Barbara, then a child of ten years, took an active part in raising funds for the Red Cross and Liberty Loan campaigns by singing patriotic songs and passing the hat. Her work was reportedly so satisfactory in Butte that officials in Helena borrowed her and repeated her success in the capital. Her public performances were limited to Red Cross drives until a theater manager booked her and started her on a professional stage career.

While in her teens, Barbara signed a motion picture contract with the Fox Film corporation, and this snippet appeared in her biography: "Barbara Luddy, the child who is credited with raising more money for Red Cross activities in 1918 than any other person of her sex in Montana, is soon to be a tuned performer in the movies, according to word received from Hollywood."

After World War I, the Luddy family removed to St. Louis, where Barbara attended school and took an active part in dramatics. After several tryouts, she was booked for a singing and dancing act on a vaudeville circuit whose route took her to Los Angeles. The 1935 March issue of *Film Comment* magazine noted that her "mother is an invalid" and that Luddy

Radio performers Barbara Luddy and Olan Soule costarred for eleven years on *The First Nighter Program*, and they also appeared together on radio programs such as Grand Hotel and Chicago Theatre of the Air. *Courtesy Great Falls Historical Society.*

found it necessary to support the family; she sought work as an extra in the Southern California motion picture studios.

While she appeared in small parts in several well-known films, Luddy found fame and a steady paycheck in voiceover work for Disney, including the voice of Lady in *Lady and the Tramp* (1955), Merryweather in *Sleeping Beauty* (1959) and Kanga in *Winnie the Pooh* shorts and television productions in the 1960s and '70s. She died of lung cancer in 1979.

HELEN LYNCH

Born April 6, 1900, Billings, Montana
Died March 2, 1965, Miami Beach, Florida

Born in Yellowstone County in 1900, Helen Lynch lost her father when she was only one year old. Her mother, Christina Fraser Lynch, moved with her two girls to Hollywood when it was a quiet, orchard-rich suburb "over the hill" from Los Angeles in 1909, three years before the first film studio arrived.

Helen's sister Agnes had bit parts in a pair of movies and later married Jason Nelson Robards Sr., which made her the custodial stepmother of actor Jason Robards Jr. and the mother-in-law of Lauren Bacall.

In 1925, Helen Lynch starred in *After Marriage* with George Fisher, and this still of the two stars from that film was used in advertisements for Durant Motors. *Courtesy Montana Historical Society.*

Helen was chosen as one of thirteen WAMPAS Baby Stars, a promotional campaign sponsored by the United States Western Association of Motion Picture Advertisers, in 1923. At the time of her screen debut, she was five feet, four inches tall, weighed 126 pounds and had blond hair and hazel eyes. She was looked on at one time as one of the screen's most promising newcomers. Her first short was in the 1918 film *Business Before Honesty* and first movie was a five-reel western titled *Showdown* with Myrtle Gonzales, George Chesebro, Edward Hearn and Art Acord. Her first leading role was in *The Other Side* with Fritzi Brunette. In 1925, she starred in *After Marriage* with George Fisher, and a still of the two stars from that film was used in advertisements for Durant Motors. During her career, she was mostly cast in comedies, something that, according to one film source, "would cause conflict between her and the directors and producers, for she wished to act in more dramatic roles, although still maintaining a great talent for provoking laughter."

She acted in a number of films throughout the late 1910s and 1920s, including *Scars and Bars* (1918), *A Rag Time Romance* (1919) and *Underworld*

(1927), as well as four small roles in the 1930s, with her credits ranging from "a speakeasy patron" to "the flirting woman on the train." It appears she returned one last time to the screen in the 1940 film *Women without Names*. During World War II, she worked as an inspector in an aircraft manufacturing plant.

A brief reference to Lynch, who is credited with fifty-seven films, appears in Oxford dictionary of film studies: "Tousle-haired silent screen comedienne and beauty contest winner, in films from 1918. Little heard from after the coming of sound. She was born in Billings, Montana, where she was also raised. After winning a beauty contest conducted in her hometown, she soon went to movie studios and received little trouble gaining roles, starting out as an extra in 1918. The winsome young actress traveled with her mother and her dog 'Tootsie' to Hollywood from Montana to enter the lists as a screen actress"

She died on March 2, 1965, in Miami Beach, Florida.

MARY MACLANE

Born May 1, 1881, Winnipeg, Canada
Died August 6, 1929, Chicago, Illinois

Mary MacLane, controversial author and feminist, was born in Winnipeg, Manitoba, on May 1, 1881. MacLane and her family first arrived in Great Falls in 1891. The family eventually settled in Butte, and MacLane graduated from Butte High School in 1899.

In 1902, MacLane, at age nineteen, wrote an autobiographical book, *The Story of Mary MacLane*. The work describes the young woman's intense personal feelings about religion, marriage, morality and the relationships between men and women. The book quickly caused a stir throughout the nation, especially in the literary centers of the East such as New York and Boston. Butte, however, felt generally outraged by MacLane's exposé, and she used royalties from her book to escape from there shortly after its publication.

In 1909, MacLane returned to Butte and thereafter earned a contract from a motion picture company from Chicago. She wrote and starred in a movie version of one of her stories, "Men Who Have Made Love to Me." The film's producer hoped to take advantage of the "vamp craze" then in

Mary MacLane (1881–1929) wrote and starred in a 1918 movie version of one of her stories, "Men Who Have Made Love to Me." *Courtesy Butte Archives.*

fashion. However, the film—no extant copy exists—failed to produce much interest with the public, although some critics praised MacLane's performance. This was MacLane's last moment in the spotlight. She died of tuberculosis in Chicago in the late summer of 1929, alone and forgotten by the public.

WILLIAM JAMES FITZGERALD "WILL" MAHONEY

Born February 5, 1894, Helena, Montana
Died February 8, 1967, Melbourne, Victoria, Australia

Helena-born William James Fitzpatrick Mahoney found fame and fortune in Australian vaudeville and stage acting. He was born in Helena in 1894 to ranchers Michael Fitzgerald and Mary Moran. His father passed away when he was two, and his mother, who had two children—Frank and

Vaudeville star Will Mahoney, in full-length portrait, standing, facing front, waving hat in the air. *Courtesy Montana Historical Society.*

Mary—from a previous marriage, held together the family by holding several odd jobs. William and his stepbrother Frank eventually concocted a vaudeville act billed as the Mahoney Brothers and toured around United States, Mexico and Australia.

Mahoney was married three times; his third wife, actress Evie Hayes, appeared frequently in his extensive stage show productions. They immigrated to Australia and were featured on the Tivoli Circuit.

Mahoney became one of the highest-paid variety stars in Australia, acting in the film *Come Up Smiling* (1939) with his wife, and then working as theater manager of the Cremorne Theatre in Brisbane.

After World War II, Mahoney went back to the United States to revitalize his career, was nominated for a Tony Award in 1956 for a revival of *Finian's Rainbow* and two years later relocated permanently to Australia, where he played in musicals and revues and trained a new generation of performers. He died on February 8, 1967.

HARRY A. MAYO

Born March 11, 1898, Helena, Montana
Died January 6, 1964, Los Angeles, California

Another fine mystery of a man, Harry A. Mayo was born on March 11, 1898, in Helena as Ray Simpson or Ramnos Sampson. While available census records are rife with misspellings, it seems as if Harry was born to Adolph and Alma Salmonson, who were married in Helena in 1895. Adolph is listed in Helena city directories as a shoemaker, and by 1900, the young family included two sons, Arthur and Ramnos, listed under the last name as Sampson. In 1910, the family was residing in Helena, and Dad was still working as shoemaker, while Mom was running a boardinghouse at 122 Grand and working as a seamstress. After losing track of the family for several decades, the 1940 census puts Ray and his mother, Alma, in California (since at least 1935) and Adolph in a home for aged in San Joaquin, California.

Ray, or Harry Mayo, is known for his work on *The Climax* (1944) and *Around the World in 80 Days* (1956) and as a bartender in *Hotel de Paree* (1960). According to the International Movie Database, his first role was as a juror in the 1944 crime mystery *A Night of Adventure*. In 1963, the year before his death, he appeared frequently in the western television programs *Gunsmoke*,

Bonanza and *Have Gun—Will Travel*. In the 1940s, he served as chairman of the Extras Advisory Committee of the Screen Actors Guild. He died on January 6, 1964, in Los Angeles, California.

MONTIE MONTANA

Born Owen Harlan Mickel, June 21, 1910, Wolf Point, Montana
Died May 20, 1998, Los Angeles, California

"Wolf Point is not the biggest town in the state of Montana," the July 1975 issue of *Western Horseman* noted, "but it's famous beyond its size." The article went on: "One reason is that it's the home of the Wild Horse Stampede, Montana's oldest rodeo. The other is that it has a native son named Owen Harlan Mickel, who grew up as Montie Montana."

Despite his nickname, Mickel liked to joke about his inability to pinpoint precisely where he was born. While it could have been Canada, or possibly North Dakota, he eventually settled on and celebrated the notion that it was someplace in eastern Montana, around Wolf Point.

Owen's father, Edgar Owen Mickel, was a roving preacher who galloped to churches in Montana and Canada on horseback. According to Owen's memoirs, the cowboys had a nickname for such poor wandering pastors: "sky pilots." His father also herded and sold wild horses and entertained at rodeos and fairs, while his mother, Mary Edna Harlan Mickel, and grandfather (also a sky pilot) performed "whipcracker acts" at the many shindigs the family frequented in their travels.

Born on June 21, 1910, Owen was their fifth child, and he was raised predominantly around Wolf Point and Miles City, engrossed in watching his father gather and sell wild horses and ramble the rodeo circuit with "rope tricks and lantern slides."

His father taught him the "ins and outs of roping," and he would exhaust hours practicing in front of the Liberty Theater in Miles City—"the only building around that was high enough to shield the rope from the winds that raked the town," according to Owen. Eventually, he worked his way "inside the theater, sweeping the floors, learning show business," as he said, "from the bottom up."

At the age of fifteen, he earned fifteen dollars (although some articles claim that it was only five dollars) performing as a trick roper at the Miles

City Fourth of July rodeo. Riding on his horse Rex, Owen came into a Miles City arena on July 4, 1925, for his first professional paid performance. It was there he was christened with his stage name. As he rode into the arena, the announcer, as the story goes, could not recall his name and simply proclaimed, "Here's Montie from Montana, the Montana Kid."

"Montie Montana" started to appear at venues, parades and events across the West as a trick roper and trick rider, another exciting form of entertainment. He wandered out to California in 1929 and began his film career as a roper, rider, stunt double and actor.

The true-life cowboy lent his skill and intrepidness to the newly expanding medium of film. He never panned out as a top-billed western star, but in 1935, he did earn the lead role in the B western *Circle of Death*. Montie Montana, however, worked with a good number of luminaries and appeared in several of the day's classic movies, including *The Man Who Shot Liberty Valance*, a 1962 film version of the novel written by Whitefish author Dorothy Johnson, and *Two Rode Together* and *Cheyenne Autumn*. All three films were directed by John Ford.

He appeared as a minor actor or stunt rider in at least nineteen films starring, among others, Roy Rogers, Gene Autry, Jimmy Stewart, Tom Mix, Clark Gable, Bob Hope, John Wayne, Frank Sinatra, Ken Maynard, Judy Garland, Shirley Temple and fellow Montana native George Montgomery. Cowboy star Rogers once called Montie "the greatest trick roper of his time."

But perhaps his most famous exploit came during President Dwight D. Eisenhower's inauguration parade in 1953. One of his most popular tricks was to lasso an unknowing member of his audience when he was performing. Montie either asked the president's permission first or Eisenhower agreed to the stunt on the spot (two differing versions of the tale exist). However it happened, Montie rode up to the presidential reviewing stand and tossed a lasso around the standing Eisenhower.

Montie recalled in his memoirs that afterward a Secret Service man told him that "if they hadn't heard the President giving him permission to rope him he would have been a sieve." The photo with Montie's rope wrapped around Eisenhower was on front pages of newspapers nationwide. (The photo here was taken a moment before the one that showed Eisenhower fully lassoed.)

Among other stunts, Montie took his horse, Poncho Rex, to the roof of the Empire State Building to let him get a look at the New York City skyline. He later roped then California governor Ronald Reagan, a former colleague from Hollywood. "Since your boyhood on a Montana ranch," Reagan

Montie Montana at the Calgary Stampede in 1941. *Courtesy Montana Historical Society.*

affectionately said in the late 1960s, "you have demonstrated the skill and independent spirit that embodies the Western tradition that we love."

In August 1964, Montie visited the Foster Frontier Photo Gallery in Miles City and was given a photograph of his father, grandfather and grandmother taken in Miles City about 1923. His father was eleven years old at the time. The photo shows the group standing by a Model T truck with a big covered van on the back. On the sides of the van is a mural of Montana scenery and the words "Pioneer Days" emblazoned across the top. The picture was

At President Dwight D. Eisenhower's inauguration parade in 1953, Montie Montana lassoed the president on the reviewing stand. It remained his best-known stunt. That's Vice President Richard Nixon near the pillar on the right. *Courtesy Montana Historical Society.*

taken by R.C. Morrison, Miles City photographer and sign-maker, who also painted the truck.

"I'd rather have this than an Oscar," Montie told the *Billings Gazette*. "I have never seen this picture before." He told *Film Comment* magazine that he especially enjoyed working with John Wayne: "In 1975, when Wolf Point was going to honor my 50th year in show business, the town was going to fly in some of the western stars....And the Indian council came to me and said, 'We don't like that you've invited Wayne. In the movies, John Wayne kills Indians.' I said to them, 'Wayne may chase Indians in the movies, but he employs more of them than anyone else in Hollywood. They may chase each other across the screen, but afterwards, they all sit down and eat lunch together.'"

In 1985, a reporter from the *Los Angeles Daily News* visited with Montie at his home in Agua Dulce, California. The reporter noted that in the yard to the left of his farmhouse was "a bell that once stood on the grounds of the Indian mission in Wolf Point, Mont."

"When I was a kid," Montie said, "I remember hearing that bell ring." In that same interview, Montie fretted about "the future of children raised without western heroes…who taught them to be clean-living and honest and kind to animals and happy and good."

Montie proudly plugged Montana wherever he went, and he said more than once in interviews that he considered Wolf Point his home. "This is the home of the real cowboys," he said while visiting Billings in 1975. "None of the rest of the states can touch Montana for that. I've seen them all and they don't stack up to us."

Similar to Roy Rogers, Montie tirelessly toured schools and children's hospitals. He doled out laughter and gauged his success in smiles. He stayed fit and active to the end. He rode in his sixtieth and final Rose Parade in 1994 at age eighty-three and put on roping and riding shows for seventy-two years, his last one at the famed Pendleton Roundup in Oregon in 1997.

Owen Harlan Mickel died on May 20, 1998, at Henry Mayo Newhall Memorial Hospital, in Valencia, California, following complications from a series of strokes. His funeral at Oakwood Memorial Park in Chatsworth, California, included many rodeo notables, actors and stuntmen.

Montie's rose-covered coffin arrived on a horse-drawn wagon serenaded by a group performing his buddy Roy Rogers's signature song, "Happy Trails."

GEORGE MONTGOMERY

Born August 29, 1916, Cascade County, Montana
Died December 12, 2000, Rancho Mirage, California

George Montgomery Letz was born on a farm outside Great Falls on August 29, 1916. The youngest of fifteen children of a Russian immigrant family, Montgomery learned farm and ranch skills as he grew up in Brady. He lived on the family homestead and attended schools in Ledger and Conrad before the family moved to a farm nearer Great Falls. His family moved within the area many times, finally settling near Black Eagle.

Montgomery told stories of hunting gophers, rattlers and coyotes to raise money for admission to the moving picture theaters and playing hooky from school to go down to the Mint Saloon and look at the Charlie Russell paintings. "A barely interested student through grade school," Montgomery

Left: George Montgomery, from Brady, made a slew of westerns in the 1930s and later musicals and detective films. *Courtesy Great Falls Historical Society.*

Below: Actor George Montgomery Letz was born on a farm outside Great Falls on August 29, 1916. *Courtesy Montana Historical Society.*

managed to graduate from Great Falls High School in 1936 in the National Honor Society.

Montgomery said that he visited Hollywood before high school graduation, which served "to intensify his desire to act." Although he gave the University of Montana a brief try, it wasn't long before he was on his way south. On his second day in Hollywood, he was on the set of a Greta Garbo film, where he used his horse-riding skills to land a job as a stuntman.

After playing bit roles from cowboys to Indians to Cossacks, Montgomery signed to star in one of the *Lone Ranger* series. He went on to act, according to one film source, "in more than 100 films," such as *The Cowboy and the Blonde,*

Ten Gentlemen from West Point with Maureen O'Hara, *Roxie Hart* with Ginger Rogers and *Coney Island* with Betty Grable.

He starred in the 1958–60 television series *Cimarron City* and had guest roles on *Wagon Train, Hawaiian Eye, Bonanza, I Spy* and *Alias Smith and Jones*.

Montgomery married singer Dinah Shore in 1943, and they owned a large ranch at Lincoln for a number of years before divorcing in 1962.

The brawny leading man died of a heart attack on December 12, 2000, at his home in Rancho Mirage, California. He was eighty-four.

JOHN P. MORSE

Born November 16, 1895, Anaconda, Montana
Died May 19, 1962, Missoula, Montana

John Park Morse was an actor who was born in Anaconda, and unlike many entertainers who find the taste of good fortune and pleasant climate in Hollywood too hard to ever part with, he returned to Montana after retiring from the industry. His film work includes roles in *Shore Acres* (1920), *Dangerous to Men* (1920) and *The Trail of the Law* (1924).

Morse was born to the earliest Anaconda residents and attended its local schools, graduated from Anaconda High School and attended Gonzaga University in Spokane. He entered theater entertainment at the age of fifteen. He played many circuits in the New England states, the Midwest and on the Pacific coast. His draft card at age twenty-one lists him as "short," with hazel eyes, and his home address as 816 Walnut in Philadelphia. The draft card stated that he was employed as an actor in Philly for the Ted Reilly Prod. Company.

After years of working as an actor and comedian in vaudeville in California, as well as getting married, he abandoned acting and returned to Montana to open a candy store in the 200 block on Main in his hometown of Anaconda. For several years, he was proprietor of a miniature golf course in the 200 block on Hickory and was the proprietor of the only duckpin bowling establishment in Anaconda. He was a member of the Methodist Church and a forty-six-year member of the Anaconda Elks Lodge. He died on May 19, 1962, in Missoula.

JAMES C. MORTON

Born August 25, 1884, Helena, Montana
Died October 24, 1942, Hollywood, Los Angeles, California

Helena-born James Carmody Lankton arrived in Hollywood in 1912 after years of vaudeville and Broadway experience, notably in the title role of L. Frank Baum's musical *The Tik-Tok Man of Oz* (1913) and as Zingo in a revival of Kalman's operetta *Countess Maritza* (1928). The balding character actor logged 209 credits, often for Hal Roach, between 1912 and 1943. Morton became a familiar face in scores of 1930s comedies, often in support of Laurel and Hardy, the Three Stooges, Our Gang and W.C. Fields, playing short-tempered policemen, irate motorists, judges, clueless druggists, court officers and bartenders. When he wasn't playing bewildered cops, waiters or bartenders, he was sporting ugly toupees that never remained on his bald head for long. (In the 1936 Three Stooges short called *Disorder in the Court*, one of his grotesque rugs is mistaken for a tarantula). In 1940, Morton returned to the stage and toured the United States in the popular Laurel and Hardy Revue. According to *The Encyclopedia of Vaudeville*, "for many years James J. Morton, billed as 'The Boy Comic' feuded with another vaudeville act, James C. Morton, who also worked at Morton and Moore, and spent large sums of money advertising in the trade papers that he was James J. Morton."

KEN NILES

Born December 9, 1906, Livingston, Montana
Died October 31, 1988, Santa Monica, California

At one time the lightweight boxing champion of Montana and an aeronautics school instructor, Ken Niles started a career on the air as an orchestra leader in Seattle in 1923. Although he spent his career almost exclusively as a pioneer broadcaster, he acted in several films in the 1930 and '40s. His most notable film role was the lawyer Leonard Eels in *Out of the Past* (1947) with Robert Mitchum. Ken began a series of original radio dramas called *Theater of the Mind* in 1928. In the mid-1930s, he was the producer and host, with Louella Parsons, of *Hollywood Hotel*, a variety show that featured interviews with movie stars and introduced the song "Hooray for Hollywood."

Ken's brother, Wendell (born in 1904 in Twin Valley, Minnesota), was one of the well-known announcers of the American golden age of radio. He was an announcer on such shows as *The Charlotte Greenwood Show*, *Hedda Hopper's Hollywood*, *The Adventures of Philip Marlowe*, *The Man Called X*, *The Bob Hope Show*, *The Burns & Allen Show*, *The Milton Berle Show* and *The Chase and Sanborn Hour*.

Ken and Miles developed one of the first radio dramas, which eventually became *Theatre of the Mind*. Wendell toured with Bob Hope during World War II and narrated a 1936 Academy Award–winning short film on the life of tennis great Bill Tilden. Among his film credits is *Knute Rockne, All American* with Ronald Reagan. Wendell was also the original announcer for *Let's Make a Deal* during that show's first season in 1963 and 1964.

Ken and Wendell are the first brothers to have stars on the Hollywood Walk of Fame.

LESLIE K. O'PACE

Born October 20, 1909, Bozeman, Montana
Died October 30, 1985, Los Angeles, California

Bozeman-born Leslie Kenneth O'Pace was an actor known for his parts as Professor Mines in *Dick Tracy* (1951–52), Peter in *Flying Leathernecks* (1951) and Preston in *Man of Conflict* (1953). He died on October 30, 1985, in Los Angeles.

JACK PADJAN

Born December 14, 1887, Silver Bow County, Montana
Died February 1, 1960, Riverside, California

Part Irish, part Blackfeet Indian, stuntman Jack Padjan (or Padjeon, as it was sometimes spelled) remains one of the more elusive cowboy actors of the 1920s and '30s. Much of his background is lost to history.

Part Irish, part Blackfeet Indian, stuntman Jack Padjan remains one of the more elusive cowboy actors of the 1920s and '30s. *Courtesy Early Film Academy.*

Jack Padjan joined the rank of top-list "Class A" western stars with *The Land of the Lawless* (1927) and *Crashing Through* (1928). *Courtesy Early Film Academy.*

©1928 Ex. Sup. Co., Chgo. Made in U.S.A.

Born in Silver Bow County, Montana, Jack Padjan was noted as an "excellent stunt rider horseman" and "formerly the champion bronco buster of the world" when he started performing in movies in the 1920s. *Courtesy Western Silent Era Film Association.*

Born in Silver Bow County, Montana, he was noted as an "excellent stunt rider horseman" and "formerly the champion bronco buster of the world" when he started performing in movies in the 1920s.

Padjan first turns up as a horseman stunt rider in the 1923 film epic *The Ten Commandments*. The following year, Padjan played Wild Bill Hickok in John Ford's *The Iron Horse* and worked with Ford again in *Three Badmen* (1926). Padjan finally joined the rank of top-list "Class A" western stars with *The Land of the Lawless* (1927) and *Crashing Through* (1928), but then he was back to smaller bit parts such as the British lancer in *The Lives of a Bengel Lancer* (1935), a part in which he was badly injured during a stunt fall; movie theater brawlers; pioneers; and henchmen. He was the stunt coordinator of *The Big Trail* (1930), which was partly filmed in Montana and featured newcomer John Wayne, a fledgling actor whom Padjan advised on the safe theatrics of stunt work.

Jack Padjan was the stunt coordinator of *The Big Trail* (1930), which was partly filmed in Montana and featured newcomer John Wayne, a fledgling actor whom Padjan advised on the safe theatrics of stunt work. *Courtesy Western Silent Era Film Association.*

He continued his work as a stunt rider and played the odd supporting role—occasionally billed as Jack Duane (like he was in the 1929 film *Redskin*)—through 1937, when he retired to run a stable in Northridge, California.

In 1957, he sued the estates of his deceased employer, Walter G. McCarty, asking $48,000 on his claim that McCarty did not keep a promise to remember Padjan in his will. Padjan managed McCarty's Rolling Hills Farm at Chatsworth, California, as a horse trainer for fifteen years. In the lawsuit, Padjan said that he worked for $400 per month but his services were worth at least $900 per month, and he would not have kept the job except for the alleged promise.

He died on February 1, 1960, in Riverside, California.

This reference to Padjan in advance of the screening of *The Land of the Lawless* in the April 6, 1928 edition of the *Burlington Hawk Eye* is perhaps about as lengthy a piece as Padjan received in print in his career: "Queer things happen in the motion picture industry. It hasn't been many years since Jack Padjan was born on a cow ranch south of Butte, Montana. As he grew into young manhood, Jack developed into an all around cowboy and in the course of time, became a champion bronco buster. While all this was in progress, Jack kept a promise made to his mother that he would never gamble with the result that he hardly knows one playing card from another. His ambition was to become a typical American stock rancher."

JOE RICKSON

Born September 6, 1880, Clearcreek, Montana
Died January 8, 1958, Los Angeles County, California

Another tantalizing enigma, Joe Rickson was born in Montana in 1880 and ended up appearing in nearly one hundred films between 1913 and 1953. His parts were relegated to small roles as henchman, homesteader, card dealer, townsman, ranch hand or a member of the gendarmes. The 1914 film *The Price of Crime* stands as his first confirmed screen credit, and his final film role was a part in director John Ford's 1953 *The Sun Shines Bright*.

FRITZI RIDGEWAY

Born April 8, 1898, Missoula, Montana
Died March 29, 1969, Palm Springs, California

Born in Missoula as Fredricke Berneice Hawkes, Fritzi Ridgeway grew up in Butte, where one newspaper writer prophesied her success: "Back there at Butte—she was one of the most popular girls in the high school, vivacious, colorful and attractive then as now, and exceedingly clever. She won state declamation contests."

The five-foot-five, 120-pound, brown-haired, blue-eyed, tomboyish "cowgirl star" Fritzi Ridgeway entered films in 1916. *Courtesy Missoula Historical Society.*

While Robert Emmet Sherwood in *The Best Moving Pictures of 1922–23 and Other Film Yearbooks of the American Screen* stated that Ridgeway was born in Butte, the majority of published sources list Ridgeway's birthdate as April 8, 1898, in Missoula, Montana.

A former trick rider, Fritzi eventually left Montana and ended up in Hollywood as a silent screen actress, where she starred in two-reel westerns and played second leads in films with Paramount Realart in the '20s. The five-foot-five, 120-pound, brown-haired, blue-eyed, tomboyish "cowgirl star" entered films in 1916. Appearing in fifty-four films between 1916 and 1934 as everything from the "attractive young church organist" to the politician's daughter, half of her film work was done between 1916 and 1919 before the introduction of sound.

She and Bob Burns (also born in Montana, in 1884) made fourteen or fifteen two-reelers for Capital in 1920 and 1921. Ridgeway's roles were usually supporting parts, mostly villainous.

In *A Woman's Vengeance,* a 1920 Capital short seventeen minutes in length, a hoard of bandits jump a mining claim belonging to Fritzi's father, and she takes the law into her own hands, strapping on a gun and chasing after the gang. She also manages to rescue her lover (Bob Burns) from the gang's plot to drown him.

Fritzi also co-starred in westerns with Roy Stewart, Harry Carey, Fred Church and Tom Mix. She married and later divorced composer Constantin Bakaleinikoff. Unable to resume her career after the arrival of sound pictures, in 1928 she built the pueblo-style Hotel del Tahquitz in Palm Springs, California.

In May 1930, Ridgeway got into trouble with the City of Los Angeles and had to put up an eight-foot fence around her 2836 Beachwood Drive home to stop her "vicious dog, Volk, an Alaskan malamute" from attacking her neighbors.

Fritzi managed the Del Tarquez Hotel in Palm Springs, California, where she was replaced for incompetence and because "she'd shoot at trespassers with a shotgun." She died of a heart attack in California on March 29, 1969.

There is one other actor-entertainer from Missoula who arrived in Hollywood earlier than Fritzi did: Earl H. Howell, who was born in 1883 and acted in several films, among them *He Met the Champion* (1910), *The Sheriff's Sacrifice* (1910) and *The Ranger's Bride* (1910). Howell died on July 18, 1918, in Boston, Massachusetts.

BURTIS "BERT" RUMSEY

Born October 15, 1898, Butte, Montana
Died July 6, 1968, Los Angeles, California

Burtis Harwood Rumsey III was born in Butte, Montana, on October 15, 1898, to Burtis Harwood Rumsey Jr. and Hannah Cummins. Hannah married Burtis, a Butte miner, on March 30, 1898, in Silver Bow County; family history says that she left him for another man, and he found her in a Seattle hotel, shot her and then killed himself. The murder-suicide took place on July 24, 1909. Their three children—Burtis, Roscoe (aka "Jim") and Doris—were left orphaned. Burtis Sr., a Civil War veteran of the Eleventh Iowa Infantry, and his wife, Margaret, raised their grandsons, while their granddaughter was raised elsewhere. The 1910 U.S. Census lists Burtis III and his brother, Roscoe, as residing with their grandparents in South Medford, Oregon.

Rumsey is most remembered for his role as Sam Noonan, the bartender, on the television western series *Gunsmoke*, the second-longest-running scripted primetime TV series in U.S. history, lasting twenty seasons. Rumsey appeared from 1956 to 1959.

Rumsey's other notable roles include the films *Botany Bay* (1953), *Desert Hell* (1958), *The Girl in Lovers Lane* (1959), *The Threat* (1960) and *Ship of Fools* (1965), as well as a television guest appearance on *The Cisco Kid*.

He died on July 6, 1968, at Woodland Hills, California, and is buried nearby at the Cherokee Memorial Park Cemetery in Lodi.

GRANT SEWELL

Born February 13, 1920, Teton County, Montana
Died May 21, 1998, Los Angeles, California

Montana-born Grant Laverne Sewell acted in small roles in television in the 1950s and '60s, including *You Are There* (1953) and *Get Smart* (1965).

RICHARD DAVIS "CHIEF" THUNDERBIRD

Born August 6, 1866, as Richard Davis Thunderbird, Tongue River, Montana
Died April 6, 1946, Los Angeles, California

Chief Thunderbird, known also as Richard Davis, was the son of Bull Bear, a Cheyenne Dog Soldier chief. Chief Thunderbird attended the Carlisle Indian School and is most known for his acting work on *Laughing Boy* (1934), *Annie Oakley* (1935) and *Silly Billies* (1936).

The *San Francisco Chronicle* reported that "the appearance of Indian actor Chief Thunderbird in Silly Billies elicited much media coverage.... Today it is impossible to fathom the hullabaloo over his appearance; the superannuated duffer grunts his dull way through five minutes of screen time."

All total, Chief Thunderbird was featured in twenty films, and his last major credited film came in 1937, where he played Chief Red Hatchet in *Wild West Days*. Similar to almost all westerns of the era, Thunderbird played the part of the villain. Directed by Ford Beebe and Clifford Smith, in *Wild West Days* the Indians plotted alongside a group known as the Secret Seven to take over the Munro Ranch.

Thunderbird made his last appearance in 1944 in the film *The Falcon Out West*, where he was uncredited in the role of Eagle Feather. He died two years later.

BESS K. TRUE

Born 1899–1901, Anaconda, Montana
Died July 9, 1947, New York City, New York

Bess K. True was, according to varying data, born in either 1899, or "about 1900," or perhaps even 1901, in Anaconda, Montana, as Laurie Flateau or a slight spelling variation thereof. She was an actress, known for *Ain't We Got Fun* (1927), *Fighting Fools* (1926) and *Strictly Kosher* (1926). According to the 1930 U.S. Census, she was living on Taft Avenue in an apartment in Los Angeles. Her father's birthplace is listed as Scotland and her mother's as Pennsylvania. Her occupation and industry are listed as actress and screen, respectively. The only other household member was nine-year-old Joseph E. True, whose birthplace is cited as Wyoming. Joseph's unnamed father's birthplace is listed as Montana. The only other reference to True outside of her stage and film appearances comes from passenger and crew lists arriving on vessels at New York City. On August 17, 1931, True, listed as age thirty, arrived from Hamilton, Bermuda, at the port of New York City, New York, on a ship named *Veendam*. Another tantalizing near-complete mystery, True died on July 9, 1947, in New York City.

MARK TWAIN

In 1861, Mississippi riverboat pilot Samuel Langhorne Clemens hopped on a stagecoach for Nevada, intending to spend a few months digging for silver. Seven years later, he emerged as "Mark Twain." On July 31, 1895, author-humorist Mark Twain, at the age of fifty-nine, arrived in Great Falls to begin a weeklong lecture tour of the state. Twain's ninety-minute program, derived from his journaling, contained such items as anecdotal references to his "two hot scotches every morning to prevent toothache" and his efforts "to quit smoking." In addition to Great Falls, Twain lectured in Butte, Anaconda, Helena and Missoula. Twain was the guest of honor at the Montana Club in Helena and was pleased with his visit, writing in his diary how he enjoyed the Butte audience, "intellectual and dressed in perfect taste—London, Parisian, New York audience—out in the mines." The Montana lectures were a small part of a five-year-long worldwide tour designed to rectify Twain's bankruptcy problems. Twain would not return to the United States until 1900.

KATHLYN WILLIAMS

Born May 31, 1879, Butte, Montana
Died September 23, 1960, Hollywood, California

Kathlyn Williams pioneered Montana into film fame. She is claimed for Butte, the copper metropolis, but her habitat was at Centerville, a well-known suburb that cuddles on a slope of the richest hill on earth at Butte's northern edge.

According to a 1925 edition of the *Los Angeles Times*, "In girlhood days, she put on concerts in one of Uncle Dick's theaters and he, characteristically, did all he could to help them along. She had a beautiful voice that attracted attention. Uncle Dick was not surprised at her conquest of fame. He said she took real intellect, remarkable fineness of character, wholesome ambition into the pictures."

She was educated at Montana Wesleyan University at Helena and at the New York School of Dramatic Art. Besides her wonderful ability as an actress and a trainer of wild animals, Williams had a beautiful soprano voice, which was once cultivated for grand opera and with which she frequently entertained her friends and studio associates. Williams's name is listed in the oration commencement exercises of the Montana Wesleyan University academy department, May 28, 1901, and as part of the school's home oratorical concert, April 14, 1900.

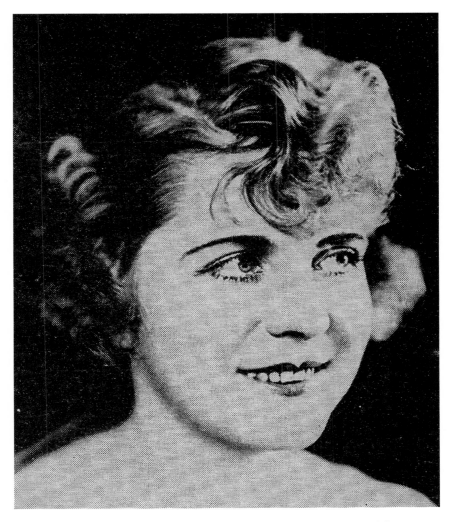

Pioneer film actress Kathlyn Williams was born in Butte and educated at Montana Wesleyan University at Helena and at the New York School of Dramatic Art. *Courtesy Butte Archives.*

Her biography on the rear side of a tobacco trading card summed up her contemporary charm and appeal: "Kathlyn Williams, a beautiful leading lady for Selig, who never hesitates to risk her life when some daring scene is called for by the scenario, was born in Butte, Montana. Her work for the last six years with the Selig Jungle Zoo animals has made her famous in 'The Adventures of Kathlyn,' but her dramatic parts in 'The Rosary,' 'The Spoilers,' 'The Ne'er

Kathlyn Williams's dramatic parts in *The Rosary*, *The Spoilers*, *The Ne'er Do Well* and *The Carpet from Bagdad* won her the distinction of being one of the foremost character actresses of silent drama. *Courtesy Silent Film Association of Hollywood.*

Do Well,' 'The Carpet from Bagdad,' have won her the distinction of being one of the foremost character actresses of silent drama."

Some of her success may be attributed to the largesse of Montana copper king William A. Clark. Born in 1839, Clark began his career as a miner, but his determination rendered him one of the most moneyed men in America and elevated him to the U.S. Senate. Clark shocked the nation by announcing his clandestine marriage to a working-class woman from Butte, Anna LaChapelle, nearly forty years his junior.

Throughout the early years of his relationship with LaChapelle, rumors of Clark's secret romances with other young women swirled, in part due to his constant sponsorship of aspiring young female artists. (It was "common knowledge in Butte that Clark had a roving eye for ladies," according to one of Clark's biographers.) Among those who benefited from his generosity was Williams, who studied and trained in both opera and acting in New York at Clark's expense. Clark also provided financial support to Margo Duffet, who became a stage actress in southern California and an early vaudeville performer in the late 1910s.

THOMAS WILSON

Born August 27, 1880, Helena, Montana
Died February 19, 1965, Los Angeles, California

Thomas Henry Wilson was born on August 27, 1880, in Helena. His father, also Thomas, was born in England, and his mother Christine's birthplace was Sweden. A copy of his "delayed birth registration" from 1942 reveals a baptismal certificate signed by Mahlon N. Gilbert, rector, St. Peter's Episcopal Church, Helena, stating that he was baptized on January 4, 1881, as well as two honorable discharges from the United States Army. In the 1900 U.S. Census, Wilson, a private in the U.S. Army, is noted as living in Athens, Illinois, with his stepfather, Elias Bengston, and mother, Christine.

His U.S. World War I draft registration card lists his residence (owned) as 1352 Spaulding Avenue in Los Angeles and his occupation as "moving pictures actor." Wilson was noted for his solid physique, rugged face and towering presence. In his youth, he boxed under the name of "Sailor"

Thomas Wilson, from Helena, played mostly bit parts through his fifty-year career, including a mustachioed policeman in Charlie Chaplin's *The Kid* (1921). *Courtesy Western Silent Era Film Association.*

Tom Wilson and once purportedly trained boxing heavyweight champion Bob Fitzsimmons.

Following his military service, Wilson found work on the vaudeville circuits and continued his training as a pugilist. According to one early film biography source, "He specialized in portraying black characters, for which roles he would use makeup made out of burnt cork and sometimes hairpieces that made him look as if he had an edging of white hair."

He appeared in 254 films between 1915 and 1963. Wilson had notable supporting roles in the silent era, like the Stonemans' blackface servant in *Birth of a Nation*, "the kindly officer" in D.W. Griffith's epic *Intolerance: Love's Struggle throughout the Ages* (1916), *Shoulder Arms* (1918), the angry policeman in Charlie Chaplin's sentimental slapstick *The Kid* (1921) and a boxing coach in Buster Keaton's comedy *Battling Butler* (1926). "His appearance in Charlie Chaplin's The Kid was off-type and without any of his usual makeup," notes one silent era film history book.

In 1928, the *Helena Daily Independent* dedicated a large spread to the film *Madam Behave* and its star, "the world's most famous woman impersonator," Butte native Julian Eltinge. The paper noted that the comedy served a cast that included "several well known screen comedians," including Tom Wilson, "a native of Helena."

After the rise of sound film, he was reduced to small roles for the rest of his extensive film career. He died on February 19, 1965, in Los Angeles, California.

BORN BETWEEN 1911 AND 1960

MARGARET ADDEN

Born June 18, 1918, Glasgow, Montana
Died January 10, 2008, San Clemente, California

Born in Glasgow, Montana, in 1918, Constance Margaret Adden was an actress known for her small part as the elevator girl in the romantic comedy *Swing Shift Maisie* (1943), *Bathing Beauty* (1944) and *See Here, Private Hargrove* (1944). Born to Herbert and Carrie Adden, available census records list her family home on Third Avenue South in Glasgow in 1920. Herbert worked as an abstracter and apparently moved the family frequently, as the Adden family lived in Spanaway, Washington, in 1930 and in Los Angeles by 1940. She died on January 10, 2008, in San Clemente, California.

STANLEY ANDERSON

Born October 23, 1939, Billings, Montana

Character actor Stanley Anderson was born in Billings in 1939 and grew up in a succession of ranch communities in eastern Montana—Billings, Red Lodge and Customs. His parents had an "on-again, off-again marriage,"

Character actor Stanley Anderson was born in Billings in 1939 and grew up in a succession of ranch communities in eastern Montana, including Billings, Red Lodge and Customs. *Courtesy Montana Film Office.*

and when it was "off for good," he was sent to live with grandparents or various aunts and uncles.

"I was in a lot of different milieu as a child and I had to try to find ways of fitting into what were usually large families wherever I went," he told the *Washington Post* in 1989. "I was a stutterer and extremely shy. I don't remember having a lot of close friends. I trace the acting impulse back to that—being very private and living a lot in the imagination."

Because of his stuttering, he was ordered to take public speaking in high school, and although he "hardly spoke to anyone," a teacher persuaded him to read Shakespeare, delve into acting and audition for plays. He found that when he was performing in plays, he "never felt I was in jeopardy," he later told the *Los Angeles Times*.

Anderson started his theatrical career at the Miller Pioneer Playhouse in the Magic City, playing the part of angels and other supporting types. He served two years of military duty in Korea, and after working for many years in repertory theaters across the country, Anderson started earning film roles. One of his first credited roles, according to the International Movie Database, was in the Montana-made *Son of the Morning Star* television miniseries in 1991. His films include *Deceived*, *RoboCop 3* and *The Pelican Brief*, and his television credits include the role of Judge Vandelay in the Seinfeld episode "The Finale."

The recurring role of George Carey, Drew Carey's father on *The Drew Carey Show*, brought him his most well-known work. His most recent acting credit comes from a small part in the television series *NYPD Blue* in 2005.

In a 1989 article in the *Washington Post* titled "The Many Faces of Stanley Anderson," he said that he embraced the concept of the character actor. "I've never believed there was a role I couldn't do," Anderson said. "Don't misunderstand. I'm not saying I could do it well. But I'm a character actor. I think in terms of character. It's all I've ever done. For me, the fun is finding the idiosyncrasies, the body shape, the internal workings of a role. I'm fascinated by the differences between the public person and the private individual. If anything runs through all my work, I've a feeling that's the thread."

NORMA ASHBY

Born December 27, 1935, Helena, Montana

Norma Ashby's television show, *Today in Montana*, first aired on station KRTV in Great Falls in 1962. Ashby served as host and producer of the television show, interviewing Montana residents and covering a wide range of Montana events. A fourth-generation Montanan, she produced more than twenty-one

Norma Ashby's television show, *Today in Montana*, first aired on station KRTV in Great Falls in 1962 and was produced up until 1988. *Courtesy Norma Ashby.*

television documentaries and interviewed more than twenty-six thousand individuals, including a number of nationally known musicians, celebrities and political figures, including Clint Eastwood, Bob Hope and Pat Nixon. The show ended in 1988.

LUCILLE BALL

Born August 6, 1911, Jamestown, New York
Died April 26, 1989, Los Angeles, California

Even today, *I Love Lucy* is syndicated all over the world, and new audiences are discovering the lure of Lucy's slapstick antics.

Before she was Lucy, Lucille Ball was "the dreamy-eyed and easily frightened child" of a telephone electrical lineman, Henry Ball, who worked gruelingly in Montana for several years. Putting telephones through Montana was brutal, even deadly work. With its mountainous territory and relentless winters, the state required fortified nerves in its telephone men.

Indeed, Ball's family epitomized America's progress from the farming age to the era of mass industry, the telegraph and the telephone. Her great-grandparents on her father's side, Clinton and Cynthia Ball, were farmers in Fredonia, New York; in 1890, they moved to the rural community of Busti, southwest of Buffalo. Their second son and fifth child, Jasper, "who was restless and bored with life on the farm," became excited by the idea of the new discovery known as the telephone. Inspired by the model of Alexander Graham Bell, he persuaded his father, Clinton, to finance him in establishing the first telephone exchange in Busti. This was in 1891, only one year after his parents bought the farm (Clinton died in 1893).

Jasper was married to Nellie, daughter of the "well-paid superintendant" of the Brooks Locomotive Works in Dunkirk, New York, and the result was that the young couple was able to build a homestead, a farm rivaling Clinton's, that "boasted one of the largest apple orchards in New York State." Unfortunately, the property burned to the ground in 1906. Jasper without delay built another farm, installing the electricity and telephone wires himself; "restless and energetic, [he] suddenly left the company

When Lucille Ball was one year old, her family moved from Anaconda to Wyandotte, Michigan, located a few miles south of the industrial center of Detroit. She often later claimed Butte as her birthplace. *Courtesy Montana Historical Society.*

in the hands of colleagues and took off for Missoula, Montana," where he started another firm with a correspondent company in Anaconda, just twenty-five miles from Butte. He had five children; his second son, Henry, then in his late teens, apparently shared his father's enthusiasm for telephone work and learned the business from the ground up by acting as an electrical lineman for Jasper.

Jasper, Henry and the other men (including Henry's brother, Frank) had to pound their way through the mouth of blizzards with, as Jasper would journal, "icicles suspended from their mustaches"; they had to carry shovels in front of their faces to allow them to breathe. The Montana snow packed as hard as marble, and at distances of a mere twelve feet, the members of the Ball team couldn't see one another. A misstep could mean a possibly fatal fifty-foot fall to the cold ground; touching an electrical wire that ran along the telephone cable could kill instantly.

Jasper grew weary of the work; he returned to Busti and then to Jamestown shortly before his granddaughter Lucy was born, while Henry kept to the job and his base in Anaconda, headquarters of the well-recognized Anaconda Copper Company, which supplied much of the wire the Ball Company used. Henry lived first at 300 Hickory Street and then at 120 West Park Avenue; both apartments were "located on thoroughfares filled with the sound of clanking streetcars and the cries of street vendors," according to Jim Brochu's *Lucy in the Afternoon: An Intimate Memoir of Lucille Ball.*

In August 1910, Henry went east to marry the pretty and lively Desiree (DeDe) Evelyn Hunt, daughter of Frederick and Florabelle Hunt of 38 Hall Avenue, Jamestown. The wedding took place on August 31 at the bride's parents' home.

The couple had no honeymoon but left at once for Anaconda so that Henry could resume work for Jasper's company while Jasper remained in Busti. In November 1910, while they were in Anaconda, sometimes going to the larger town of Butte for shopping or visits to the theater, DeDe became pregnant. In the tradition of the time, according to Brochu, "DeDe wanted to have her baby in her hometown," and the couple returned there briefly. No sooner was Lucy born, on August 6, 1911, than Henry, DeDe and their child moved back to Anaconda, "where they took an apartment on noisy, dusty Commercial Avenue in the downtown section [on the southwest corner of Oak Street]."

At least one of Ball's biographers went so far as to blame "ugly and commercial" Anaconda as the source of the famous entertainer's "lifelong issues with chronic nervousness and anxiety": "Lucy's first impressions of life were of the cramped, flat, ugly little town dominated by the Anaconda Copper Company's smoke-belching chimneys of blackened brick. The constant clanging of the streetcar was the dominant sound of her babyhood. Her mother's tension over Henry's dangerous work was another feature that influenced Lucy. Throughout her life, from childhood on, she was extremely tense, nervous, sensitive, and vulnerable, filled with anxiety and fear."

Because Butte was the commercial hub of that region, Ball for many years believed that she was born there, an understandable assumption that led many journalists to accuse her of inventing her birthplace. A number of magazines reported inaccurately that she had decided that Montana was "a more romantic place" to be born than New York State and thus created a whimsy of a "Western childhood."

When Ball was one year old, the family moved to Wyandotte, Michigan, located a few miles south of the industrial center of Detroit. Ball's father died of typhoid fever when she was three years old, and she later became the victim of her stepfather's parents, who would "literally chain her to a leash in the backyard."

According to one biographer, she became interested in her family history and "wrote to the Chamber of Commerce in Anaconda and Butte for informational pamphlets and then soon knew more about the towns than probably many people who actually lived there."

When Ball went to the New York in the 1920s, she began telling people that she was from Montana and continued to publicly state she was from Montana for many years after. This unlikely candidate—the daughter of a lineman in Anaconda and elsewhere—would become the country's most famous comedienne and truly a television pioneer.

On April 26, 1989, she died from a ruptured aorta following open-heart surgery at Cedars-Sinai Medical Center in Los Angeles.

DIRK BENEDICT (DIRK NIEWOEHNER)

Born March 1, 1945, Helena, Montana

Born Dirk Niewoehner in Helena on March 1, 1945, Dirk Benedict led a tranquil childhood of fishing, skiing and grouse hunting in White Sulphur Springs, the county seat of Meagher County.

Benedict said that he "had the childhood that Hemingway wrote about. We knocked around on our own, made bows and arrows and hunted, floated the Smith River, and fished and fished and fished. We didn't have television until the '60s and the movie theater was only open in the summer." When he was sixteen, however, his parents divorced. And when Dirk was eighteen, his father, George, died.

"My dad always taught me that life wasn't just about going through the motions," said Benedict, seventy-two. "He was interested with the discovery of what gave each life its real and unique qualities. That made such an impression."

Football was among Dirk's earliest interests—he spent summer evenings playing catch with George. He dreamed of playing college football until he auditioned "on a prank and a bet" for the spring musical at Whitman College, in Walla Walla, Washington, earning the lead in a production of Oscar Hammerstein's *Show Boat.*

"Never once when I was stacking hay in the high mountain hayfields of Montana did I daydream about being any kind of celebrity," said Benedict. "Even in my college years and beyond, I considered it playacting, fun, just sort of a hobby."

He advanced his acting studies through a two-year apprentice program in Michigan and began appearing in repertory productions all over the country.

During this period, he adopted his stage surname—inspired by a breakfast of eggs Benedict with his agent. While looking down at the two halves of an English muffin, topped with ham, poached eggs and Hollandaise sauce, he decided he would become "Dirk Benedict."

Dirk Benedict made his Broadway debut in 1971 before launching his onscreen career with the little-known Swedish drama *Georgia, Georgia.* Benedict's breakthrough happened in 1978 at age thirty-three, cast as Lieutenant Starbuck on producer Glen A. Larson's television space opera *Battlestar Galactica,* a $14 million, three-hour epic for ABC.

115

White Sulphur Springs' Dirk Benedict is best known for playing the characters Lieutenant Templeton "Faceman" Peck in *The A-Team* television series and Lieutenant Starbuck in the original *Battlestar Galactica* film and television series. *Courtesy Dirk Benedict.*

A memorable scoundrel with a fondness for card games and the ladies, Starbuck was the most skilled pilot in the Galactica fleet. Benedict's good looks and self-belittling sense of humor made for a memorable character. The show was canceled in 1979. After *Galactica*, Benedict appeared in many forgettable features and programs before landing his most popular part as Templeton "Faceman" Peck on *The A-Team*. The show, which turned Mr. T. into a household consonant, was a cartoon-like action series about four Vietnam veterans who worked as honorable soldiers for hire. "If the 'A-Team' was about anything," said Benedict, "it was about people standing up for themselves and having control of their own lives."

The A-Team brought Benedict sizeable attention during its four-year run but sank in the ratings in its fifth season. Benedict returned to episodic television. Since then, he has made his big-screen directorial debut and participated in *Bring Back...The A-Team*, a documentary that reacquainted the surviving members of the series. Benedict made a cameo in the action-comedy adaptation of *The A-Team* (2010), featuring Bradley Cooper as his former character.

These days, Benedict can be seen at comic book and collectibles shows from coast to coast. Because Benedict had reportedly made White Sulphur Springs out to be a hick town in a few interviews, he has a few detractors. "After all, I'd come from a town that had no TV or movie theater, where we used kerosene lamps and outhouses. And here I am attending operas and accepting invitations to dinner at the homes of very sophisticated people," Benedict once said. These comments reportedly raised some hackles in White Sulphur Springs.

Nonetheless, his intensely Montanan attitude to live simply has remained untouched by time and travel. "I've been fortunate to have lived a marvelous life," said Benedict, who splits his time between Kalispell, the West Coast and visiting his mother, who still lives in White Sulphur Springs. "Coming from Montana, it's been a long, long, long journey. Miracles happen in funny ways."

Brad Bird

Born September 11, 1957, Kalispell, Montana

Born in Kalispell, Brad Bird was raised in Corvallis, Oregon, where he spent his formative years. After he graduated from Corvallis High School in 1975, Disney offered Brad a scholarship to its animation program at the California Institute of the Arts.

Bird later penned the script for *batteries not included* (1987), a Steven Spielberg–produced fantasy, and also animated and directed a few episodes of *The Simpsons* during his eight-year involvement with the show.

Among his highest achievements, Bird was selected to write and direct *The Incredibles*, which received four Academy Award nominations, including Best Original Screenplay, Best Sound Editing, Best Sound Mixing and Best Animated Feature Film. It was rewarded with Best Animated Feature Film and Best Sound Editing.

Bird wrote *Ratatouille*, which opened to universal acclaim in June 2007, grossed $621 million worldwide and earned several critic's awards, a Golden Globe for Best Animated Feature and five Oscar nominations, including the Academy Award for Best Animated Feature Film.

Bird recently returned to live action with *Mission Impossible: Ghost Protocol* and *Tomorrowland*, starring George Clooney.

Rosemarie Bowe

Born September 17, 1932, Butte, Montana

Rosemarie Bowe was born on September 17, 1932, in Butte, the youngest child of Dennis and Ruby Bowe. Her father was a building contractor and construction worker, and her mother was a dress designer. The Bowe family of five moved to Tacoma, Washington, when Rosemarie was a young child.

As a teenager, she worked as a model in Seattle. At five-foot-five, with salient blue-green eyes, Bowe secured work in Los Angeles as a model, appearing in several pinup portraits by artist Gil Elvgren.

Born in Butte in 1932, Rosemarie Bowe moved in 1950 to Hollywood, where she obtained a contract with Columbia Pictures. *Courtesy Butte Archives.*

Bowe moved in 1950 to Hollywood, where she obtained a contract with Columbia Pictures. "Rosemarie Bowe is a young actress with a face like Grace Kelly and a body like Marilyn Monroe," observed a writer from the *Cumberland Sunday Times* in 1955. She appeared in several uncredited parts as a swimmer or scantily clad beauty before working her way up to larger roles, including 20th Century Fox's *The Peacemaker* (1956).

In June 1952, she appeared on the cover of *LIFE* magazine. On January 23, 1956, Bowe married actor Robert Stack in Beverly Hills Lutheran Church. Her later acting roles included appearances in the low-budget films and TV movies, some of which starred her husband.

In 1970, Bowe was in an automobile accident in Sacramento, California, and sustained serious internal injuries, which forced her to retire from show business.

BARBARA BROWER

Born February 19, 1916, Miles City, Montana
Died October 28, 1976, Riverside, California

Born in Miles City in 1916, Barbara Brower was an actress known for the role of Mary Jane in *Salomy Jane* (1923) and bit parts in *The Covered Wagon* (1923) and *The Fighting Coward* (1924).

DENNIS CROSS

Born December 17, 1924, Whitefish, Montana
Died April 6, 1991, Los Angeles, California

Born in Whitefish, Montana, on December 17, 1924, Dennis Cross joined the Marine Corps at age seventeen and fought against the Japanese at the Battle at Guadalcanal. He studied acting on the GI bill at the Actors Lab in Hollywood and ended up in New York City, where he appeared in scores of live television shows and commercials.

Dennis appeared on a Philco Television Playhouse production entitled *A Trip to Bountiful* with famous silent movie star Lillian Gish. According to a story shared by a member of the Cross family, Dennis had worked the night shift in a factory the day before the shooting of the episode and had broken one of his fingers. With his finger in a bandaged splint, he approached the producer and apologized for his injury. While he may have expected to have been sent away from taping, the opposite happened. A photo from this episode can be seen in the archives of the Museum of Modern Art, New York. The uniformed Cross stands behind the cage of a bus ticket counter, his finger in a white splint, handing over to Lillian Gish her riding pass.

When he returned to California, he co-starred in *The Osceola Story* about the Seminoles. He appeared in six episodes of *The Rifleman* as a gunslinger, cowboy and gang member and had the lead in *The Blue Angels*, a syndicated television series about the daredevil United States Navy pilots (1960–61).

When he retired from acting, he went to work as a vice-president of the Doctors Insurance Company in Santa Monica. He died in Los Angeles at age sixty-six. He is the father of former UCLA and San Francisco 49er star lineman Randy Cross.

JANE L. DRUMMOND

Born 1916, Red Lodge, Montana
Died 1967, Bridger, Montana

Red Lodge–born actress Jane L. Drummond appeared in a number of films in the 1940s, most prominently in *The Fargo Kid* (1940), *Women in Hiding* (1940) and *The Human Comedy* (1943). She first appeared onscreen in the 1940 Joan Crawford film *Susan and God*. Even the most basic details of Drummond's life are scant, including simple birth and death dates. She is buried at Bridger Cemetery in Bridger, Montana.

Red Lodge–born actress Jane L. Drummond, *far right*, appeared in a number of films in the 1940s, and she first appeared onscreen in the 1940 Joan Crawford film *Susan and God. Courtesy Red Lodge Historical Society.*

PATRICK DUFFY

Born March 17, 1949, Townsend, Montana

Actor Patrick Duffy was raised in Boulder, Montana, and told *Us Weekly* magazine in 1985, "[E]ven as a kid growing up in Boulder…I always had a certain amount of chutzpa. It's easy growing up in Montana. There aren't a lot of obstacles. Fishing in the summer. Sledding in the winter. Loving parents. And my dog, Blue. It's sort of like Norman Rockwell paintings brought to life."

After high school, Duffy enrolled in the Professional Actors Training Program at the University of Washington. Best known as Bobby Ewing on television's *Dallas*, Duffy has worked off-Broadway and had smaller roles in several movies and made-for-television movies. He is a practicing Buddhist, a faith that he said gave him the strength to cope with his parents' shooting death in Montana in November 1986. Parents Terence and Marie Duffy were killed by shotgun blasts at the tavern they owned in Boulder. Two local teenagers were convicted of the murders and sentenced to seventy-five years in prison.

Duffy, who reprised his notable role of Bobby Ewing role in a forty-episode *Dallas* revival between 2012 and 2014, is still active in television series and movie work.

JOSIP ELIC

Born March 10, 1921, Butte, Montana

Joseph Elich Jr. grew up in the Cabbage Patch, an East Side slum in Butte home to bootleggers, drunks and poor rough folks. His father, Joseph, a native of Croatia, became a U.S. citizen in 1937 at the Butte–Silver Bow County courthouse. Neither his father nor his mother, Martha, spoke English.

Josip worked the mines at age sixteen, joined the U.S. Navy and then moved to New York City after completing his tour of duty. He altered his name when he became an actor at age thirty. In 1945, prompted by his lady friend to find a different line of work other than a New York finance office worker, Josip attended acting school on the GI bill. His first role was in *Threepenny Opera* off-Broadway, which ran for ninety-six performances in 1954. While Elic appeared in several successful television programs, including *The Twilight Zone*, and films in his career, including Mel Brooks's *The Producers* (1967) and *Black Rain* (1989) with Michael Douglass, he is most known for his role in *One Flew Over the Cuckoo's Nest* (1975). In the adaptation of Ken Kesey's novel of the same name, Josip plays Bancini, a reticent mental ward inmate. According to *People*, "The scene in which star Jack Nicholson jumps on Bancini's back for a piggy back ride was ad-libbed."

In 2015, Elic visited family and friends in Butte and told the *Montana Standard* that because the "Twilight Zone Marathon" plays annually on the SyFy channel, a new generation of fans has become familiar with him. He told a reporter that he "attends Twilight Zone and science fiction conventions, to the fans' delight."

"My big autographs used to be 'Cuckoo's Nest,'" said Elic to the *Montana Standard*. "Now it's 'Twilight Zone.'"

PABLO ELVIRA

Born September 24, 1937, San Juan, Puerto Rico
Died February 5, 2000, Bozeman, Montana

Pablo Elvira grew up poor in Puerto Rico, the son of a dance orchestra leader, and he began his musical career playing trumpet in his father's group. He soared to great heights with his baritone voice. He sang in New York City's Metropolitan Opera, "the world's greatest opera house," for many years, performing with such opera greats as Joan Sutherland, Luciano Pavarotti and Placido Domingo.

During his career, Elvira sang in France, Germany, South America, Australia, Puerto Rico, Israel and throughout the United States. He became famous for singing the cocky, wisecracking part of Figaro in *The Barber of Seville*.

A meeting with the Puerto Rican cellist and conductor Pablo Casals led to his pursuing a career as an opera singer. In 1966, while participating in the Metropolitan Opera Auditions in New York, Elvira was heard by the dean of the Indiana University School of Music in Bloomington, who asked the young baritone to join the voice faculty. Elvira remained there for eight years teaching and performing.

It was there that he met his future wife, Bozeman native Signe Landoe, and they married in 1975 in New York City. They moved to Bozeman, where they built a home, in 1976. They also kept houses in other locations and had a son, also named Pablo.

The elder Pablo left Bloomington in 1974, toured and performed in Europe and then moved to New York, where he made his debut that year with City Opera as Germont in Verdi's *Traviata*. His Met debut came in 1979 as Tonio. His final Met performance was as Figaro in 1990.

In 1983, in an interview with the *Bozeman Chronicle*, he called Montana "a soothing sanctuary where he could take care of himself and rest his voice between performances." He talked of "my beautiful state of Montana" and referred conversationally to the "opera nuts" who filled the seats and made him a star. "I've been quite lucky with the critics," he said.

He sang regularly in annual operas in Montana and lent his name to the local productions. In a 1994 interview, he talked of "the difficulty of playing Figaro—every time [you] walk on stage, you have to be like a light bulb, you have to be up, boom!"

Elvira's last performance in Bozeman was in the Italian opera *Il Trovatore* in 1996. He also spearheaded the Rimrock Opera Company in Billings and performed *The Barber of Seville* there in November 1999, probably his last performance in Montana.

He died at his home in Bozeman in 2000. He was sixty-two and passed of natural causes. Pablo Elvira's "heart really was here [in Montana]," his widow told the *Bozeman Chronicle* shortly after the singer's death. There is a star emblazoned with his name in the tile in front of the Ellen Theatre in Bozeman.

DARLENE EUSTROM

Born December 17, 1930, Miles City, Montana

Born on December 17, 1930, in Miles City as Darlene Eustrom, Dee Arlen appeared in several small television and films roles, including *Leave It to Beaver* (1957), *Perry Mason* (1957) and *The Ladies Man* (1961).

According to the 1916 *City Directory of Miles City, Glendive, Terry, Sidney and Forsyth* and the 1916 *County Directory of Custer, Dawson, Prairie, Richland and Rosebud Counties*, the Eustrom family resided at 409 South Nowlan Avenue in Glendive. Roy was employed at that time as half owner of Eustrom & Sinclair produce; Mrs. Lelia Eustrom was a violinist at the Isis Theatre.

According to the 1940 U.S. Census, by the time that she was nine, Darlene Eustrom was living in El Centro, Imperial, California, with her older brother, Jack, age eighteen, and her forty-eight-year-old mother, Lelia, and fifty-one-year-old father, Roy Eustrom. Jack's birthplace is noted as Montana, and Roy's occupation is "salesman clothing" at a department store.

THOMAS "TIMMY" EVERETT

Born February 14, 1938, Helena, Montana
Died March 4, 1977, New York City, New York

Timmy Everett was born in Helena on February 14, 1938. His grandfather Charles Everett at one time worked as a janitor at the Montana Club and a cement worker, and he also owned a furniture store in Helena at 16 South Main. Timmy's father, Thomas Everett, worked at Howe's Confectionery at 122 North Rodney before opening Everett's Fountain at 800 East Sixth Avenue.

The details of Everett's transition to New York City from Montana are nebulous, but he almost certainly began his theatrical career at fourteen in a television production of *On Your Toes*. He studied at the Neighborhood Playhouse School of the Theater (a full-time professional conservatory located in New York City), and after several seasons of summer stock, he landed a dancing part in *Damn Yankees*, followed by the juvenile and dancing lead in *Reuben, Reuben*.

The actor-dancer won the Daniel Blum Theater World Award in 1957 for his supporting role as the young Jewish boy in William Inge's *The Dark at the Top of the Stairs*.

In 1958, Everett won the Theater World Award for Best Supporting Actor in *The Cold Wind and the Warm*. Of this performance, John Chapman wrote in the book *Broadway's Best, 1959*: "There was a fine performance by Timmy Everett as a lad not unlike young Behrman—on the verge of manhood but not yet sure of himself or his talent."

Everett directed and choreographed a number of Broadway plays and appeared in supporting roles in television productions. His most significant work was on the films *Rendezvous* (1957), *John Brown's Raid* (1960) and *The Music Man* (1962).

He died on March 4, 1977, in New York City, purportedly "of myocardial infarction from amphetamine addiction." He died in his sleep while he had been visiting a friend at 201 West Seventy-Seventh Street. He was thirty-eight years old and resided in California.

KAY FARRINGTON

Born July 26, 1939, Glasgow, Montana

Born in Glasgow on July 26, 1939, Kay Farrington secured small roles in several television shows, including *Bachelor Father* (1957), *The Many Loves of Dobie Gillis* (1959) and *In Like Flint* (1967).

PETER FONDA

Born February 23, 1940, New York City, New York

Born in New York City in 1939, Peter Fonda is a well-known counterculture icon of the 1960s who earned notoriety as a rebel from such films as *The Wild Angels* and *The Trip*. His first big hit was *Easy Rider*, a groundbreaking and rebelliously spirited movie that is considered a classic today. His career took a turn downward for several years until he starred in the 1997 film *Ulee's Gold*, which earned him an Academy Award nomination for best actor. He has more than seventy films to his credit.

Fonda moved to Montana to follow a woman with roots in the state in the 1970s and has made the Paradise Valley his principal residence ever since. "Yes, the move to Montana was a major change in my life," Fonda told *Rolling Stone* in 2016. "Montana is gorgeous. A celebrity can live here undisturbed."

Hatchfest, an annual international film and arts festival held in Bozeman each fall since 2004, was cofounded by Fonda and Yarrow Kramer. "We've been cowboys and ranchers, now we should pay attention to the arts. Besides, the festival brings in money. Film was a natural first choice because it is the most immediate of the arts; it grips one and takes hold of the mind. There are some excellent film people right here."

MARTIN GOOD RIDER (WILLIAM MARTIN PEPION)

Born November 13, 1924, Blackfeet Reservation, Browning, Montana
Died July 1, 1966, Montana

At age thirteen, Martin Good Rider was selected by a Fox film scout for a part in a Shirley Temple picture called *Susannah of the Mounties* (1939). The story revolves around Indian resistance to construction of the Canadian Pacific railway, presenting the Blackfeet in an overall credible light.

Good Rider's work on the 20th Century Fox picture was the result of an audition given to him with other Indian boys in New York City in the spring of 1938, when a picture of the boys watching the printing press in a New York newspaper operate came to the attention of a representative of that firm. Under sponsorship of the Marquette Legion of Indian Missions, the six Indian boys had attended the Eucharistic Congress in New Orleans and had taken part in a number of programs in New York. Of the six, Good Rider was selected to take part in a picture and the contract was signed. Members of the tribe rushed to complete the costume Good Rider wore in his role of Little Chief, as noted in *Screenplay*: "Father Bernard A. Cullen brought the boys home and immediately arranged for a war suit, moccasins war bonnet and drum to be completed by the Blackfeet Indians in one week's time. Usually a woman spends all winter making a war suit for her man, but Good Rider had to go to Hollywood at once, completely costumed in the manner of his forefathers."

Cecile Crow Feathers, one of the Blackfeet Indian WPA craft teachers, gathered ten top bead workers in the craft shop and assigned each a strip of bead work or a big sun-pattern medallion for the war suit. An old warrior was to make the war bonnet, and a young Blackfoot started work on the drum. The outfit was completed just in time for Good Rider to go to Hollywood and a possible career. He was accompanied by Father Cullen and Father Egon Mallman, the latter from the diocese at Heart Butte on the Blackfeet Reservation.

Good Rider excelled in the role of Temple's screen boyfriend, and members of the Blackfeet Indian tribe were transported to Hollywood to add authenticity to the movie. According to *Screenplay*, "In order to prevent any hitch in the arrangements made for their care, the studio posted a $25,000 bond with the Bureau of Indian Affairs. The tribesmen's

At age thirteen, Blackfeet member Martin Good Rider was selected by a Fox film scout for a part in a Shirley Temple picture called *Susannah of the Mounties* (1939). *Courtesy Montana Historical Society.*

contract stated that they be paid from the time they left Browning until their return, and that at all times should be present with them to attend to their needs."

While a newspaper clipping in 1939 referred to Good Rider heading to Hollywood to make another picture, according to IMDb, *Susannah of the Mounties* was Good Rider's first and final film. He died in a car accident in Montana in 1966.

Kirby Grant

Born November 24, 1911, Butte, Montana
Died October 30, 1985, Brevard County, Florida

Kirby Grant Hoon Jr. was born in Butte, Montana, on November 24, 1911, the son of Kirby Grant Hoon Sr. and Henrietta Divel Caldwell. The family moved to Missoula in 1936. Kirby Sr. was sales manager for the Highlander Brewing Company and later for John R. Daily Meat Company. During the 1920s, he was a nationally ranked handball player and was Montana state singles champion several times. A professional baseball player from 1901 to 1910, Mr. Hoon was appointed chairman of the first Montana State Athletic Commission by former governor John Erickson.

Young Grant was educated at the University of Washington in Seattle, Whitman College in Walla Walla, Washington, and the American Conservatory of Music. He was considered a child prodigy as a violinist. Also an accomplished singer, Grant was a radio and supper club entertainer before entering films.

Grant first made his acting reputation in film in the late 1930s. He played leads in low-budget westerns and other action pictures, often as a Canadian mountie in such movies as *Trail of the Yukon, Call of the Klondike, Northwest Territory, Yukon Gold* and *Northern Patrol.*

Grant starred in *Sky King* as the wealthy owner of the Flying Crown Ranch in Arizona. He used his airplane, *Songbird*, to fight wrongdoers. *Sky King* started as a daytime weekend show and appeared in prime time from September 1953 to September 1954. It returned to weekend daytime programming in 1959 and ran until 1966.

Grant and his wife, Carolyn, moved to Florida in the early 1970s and lived in Winter Springs, an Orlando suburb. He bought a circus in 1965 and often took leading parts in local theatrical productions, and he served as a goodwill ambassador for SeaWorld of Orlando.

Grant was killed on October 30, 1985, in a car accident while en route to watch the launch of the space shuttle *Challenger*. Grant, seventy-three, was alone at the time, traveling east on a state road at 8:00 a.m., and tried to pass the car in front of him when that vehicle also pulled out to pass. Grant swerved left onto the shoulder and then swerved back to the right and into a ditch, which contained three feet of water. A passerby pulled him out and he was taken to hospital, but he was dead on arrival.

Right: Butte-born Kirby Grant first made his acting reputation in film in the late 1930s, mostly playing leads in low-budget westerns and other action pictures. *Courtesy Butte Archives.*

Below: In the 1950s, Kirby Grant starred in *Sky King* as the wealthy owner of the Flying Crown Ranch in Arizona. He used his airplane, *Songbird*, to fight wrongdoers. *Courtesy Butte Archives.*

VIRGINIA HOGEN

Born February 11, 1914, Great Falls, Montana
Died, date unknown

Born in Great Falls, Victoria Hogen appeared in small roles in several films, including *USA* and the Walter Lang musical *Song of the Islands*, both of which were released in 1942.

RUNE H. HULTMAN

Born May 26, 1917, Missoula, Montana
Died March 26, 1998, Drummond, Montana

The son of Mr. and Mrs. Al Hultman, Rune H. Hultman grew up at 1232 East Second Street in Butte and graduated from Butte High School and the Pasadena Playhouse, a drama school in California, before enlisting as an aerial gunner in the U.S. Air Force in January 1941. During World War II, he lined his sights on the Axis powers. According to the *Butte Montana Standard* of May 16, 1943, "Once a pilot candidate, the determined Butte young man suffered a back injury in an air accident but refused a medical discharge, then turned to gunnery [of the Army Air Forces] as the next best bet to keep him flying." He served as a gunner and radio operator aboard a Flying Fortress. It appears that he started performing while in the army, playing one of the lead roles in *Winged Victory*, an Army Air Forces play that opened in Boston on November, 2, 1943.

The production then went on tour after completing its run in the Shubert Theater in Boston. The three-hour performance related the experience of six army flyers from the time they enter boot camp to combat duty in the Pacific. Hultman played the part of one of the flyers. The cast was made up of eighty members of the Army Air Forces. According to a review in the *Boston Traveler*, "Winged Tribute" is termed a glowing tribute to the Army Air Forces and a salute to democracy. One of the outstanding scenes depicts a Christmas celebration on a South Pacific island, the merry opening of packages, the hilarious entertainment and the singing of "Silent Night," with its peaceful message shattered by the scream of the alert.

After exiting the service, he studied radio at Sioux Falls, South Dakota, and later he appeared as himself in a pair of movies, the armed forces drama *Winged Victory* (1944) and the western-themed *Code of the Lawless* (1945), the latter of which starred Montana-born Kirby Grant.

CHET HUNTLEY

Born December 10, 1911, Cardwell, Montana
Died March 20, 1974, Big Sky, Montana

Saco, Montana—the kind of place where you step off into eternity and wonder if you will ever make it back. Situated along the Hi-Line, where the land lays flat and scrubby, Saco is a roughneck town of only a few hundred and home to the Chet Huntley Schoolhouse.

During the 1950s and '60s, tens of thousands of Americans tuned in every night for *The Huntley-Brinkley Report*, as Chet Huntley and David Brinkley delivered the NBC evening news.

Born in the Northern Pacific Railroad depot living quarters on December 10, 1911, in Cardwell, Montana, Huntley progressed from "the middle of nowhere" to living rooms across America through a persona bred of the Montana landscape, hard work and persistence. His father was a traveling railroad telegrapher. The Huntley family had taken up homestead farming fifteen miles north of Saco, in the Milk River Country, for about eleven years beginning in 1912.

Within a mile of the Huntley farm, the Huntley School was built. Chet started his education there. The student body, all in one room—first through eighth grade—numbered about a dozen. The Huntleys sold the Saco farm in 1924. In 1928, Chet worked for the Whitehall State Bank as a teller. The Huntley family would live in various southern Montana towns: Big Timber, Norris, Pony, Whitehall and Bozeman, to name a few.

Huntley attended college at Montana State University and the University of Washington. Beginning his broadcast career in 1934 at KPCB radio, 710-AM (now the fifty-thousand-watt KIRO), one of eight radio stations in Seattle, Huntley earned ten dollars per month. He received his crucial breakthrough as a CBS radio newscaster in the 1940s and then moved to ABC in the early 1950s.

In 1955, he joined NBC and David Brinkley for the popular *Huntley-Brinkley Report*. Airing for fourteen years, the program won seven Emmys and two George Foster Peabody Awards, and during the 1964 political convention, it achieved record-breaking Nielsen television ratings.

Despite an exceptional career in broadcasting, Huntley is also associated these days for conceptualizing construction of the Big Sky Corporation, a then $20 million skiing and real estate development south of Bozeman.

Huntley formulated the notion of Big Sky Corporation in 1968. He retired from NBC in 1970 to administer its development, which faced opposition: many Montanans didn't want unspoiled public land transformed to a resort. Huntley was paid a slice of stock (0.77 percent) for staking his reputation behind the development. He cajoled two Montana governors, obtaining permission for the resort to make use of the state's nickname, Big Sky. He garnered support from state and federal agencies and members of Congress. He flew around Montana, delivering his sales pitch to ranchers and farmers

During the 1950s and '60s, tens of thousands of Americans tuned in every night for *The Huntley-Brinkley Report*, as Saco-born Chet Huntley and David Brinkley delivered the NBC evening news.

in small towns. He shook hands and made promises of better days ahead. He found customers who purchased condos.

Huntley, though, died before the resort staged a grand opening of its ski lifts in 1974 and exerted little influence over the finished product. A heavy smoker, he died of lung cancer three days before the celebration.

Boyne USA bought Big Sky two years after Huntley's death. In 2013, Big Sky Resort and Moonlight Basin merged together to form the largest ski resort in the United States with more than 5,800 acres, more than 250 named runs and 4,350 vertical feet.

Open to visitors during the summer months, the Chet Huntley Schoolhouse evokes an insightful image of the times when he attended class there, the relic of a schoolboy who afterward successfully navigated the game of life to the heights of national prestige and influence. "Be patient and have courage—there will be better and happier news some day, if we work at it," Huntley said on his final broadcast.

EVEL KNIEVEL

Born October 17, 1938, Butte, Montana
Died November 30, 2007, Clearwater, Florida

Wearing yellow leathers and riding a Triumph motorcycle, Butte native Evel Knievel made nine appearances on ABC Television's *Wide World of Sports*. Appearing as a side attraction to an auto race, Knievel once jumped fifteen cars in Gardena, California, and most famously jumped the Caesars Palace Fountains in Las Vegas on a Harley-Davidson motorcycle. Knievel cleared the fountains but crashed on the landing ramp, suffering multiple injuries requiring a month-long stay in a hospital. Knievel became a national celebrity with his stunt on January 1, 1968.

On September 8, 1974, with incredible media fanfare, daredevil Evel Knievel tried and failed to leap the mile-wide chasm of the Snake River Canyon on his specially engineered rocket motorcycle. His drogue parachute malfunctioned and opened on takeoff. Evel and his contraption floated to the bottom of the canyon, landing on the riverbank directly below his launch ramp. Knievel later died in 2007.

ANDREA LEEDS

Born August 18, 1913, Butte, Montana
Died May 21, 1984, Palm Springs, California

Andrea Leeds was born Antoinette M. Lees to Charles E. and Lina Lees on August 18, 1913, in Butte, Montana. Leeds was the daughter of a British-born mining engineer whose interests were fleeting. Andrea was purportedly "an endearing, good natured child" and was called "Little Jupe" by the ranchers working outside Butte. The family moved to Arizona in 1918 and, after that, Long Island, where she began high school. It was around that time that she discovered an emerging talent in music, and she was sent off to Chicago to study at the conservatory and attend high school.

Her father was then sent to work in Durango, Mexico, and Andrea came along for the adventure. The country was ravaged by prevalent internal strife and dangerous for foreigners. Andrea's personal recollections were studded with bandit invasions and kidnapping scares, and she acquired a wealth of material for exciting stories. When bandits threatened her parents and said that Andrea would be kidnapped, Charles and Lina sent their daughter alone back to the United States to continue her education in Los Angeles.

During her four years at UCLA, from which she got her Bachelor of Arts degree, she studied with a writing career in mind. "After I graduated," she told *Filmplay*, "I tramped all through Los Angeles and Hollywood trying to land some sort of writing job, with no luck. I also tried writing short stories, with the same result. When I was offered an acting contract, I still tried to sell Mr. Goldwyn on the idea of hiring me as a writer. Still no luck."

Her introduction to acting came as Antoinette Lees in 1933 as a "college girl" in MGM's *Meet the Baron*, a nutty comedy about a legendary baron. She signed a contract with Samuel Goldwyn, who requested that she change her name. "Andrea Leeds" first appeared in the prestigious *Come and Get It* (1936).

Andrea was nominated for an Academy Award for Best Supporting Actress in *Stage Door* (1937), and director Gregory La Cava once called her "the best natural actress who has ever passed under my hands." That's no small compliment considering that Leeds was part of an ensemble cast in *Stage Door* that included Katharine Hepburn, Ginger Rogers and Lucille Ball.

Andrea read for the role of Melanie in *Gone with the Wind*; however, the role was given to Olivia de Havilland. Among other films, Leeds appeared as the romantic female lead opposite Montana-born Gary Cooper in *The Real Glory* (1939), an adventure film set in the Philippines in 1906, and across from Don Ameche in the first Technicolor biopic of composer Stephen Foster, *Swanee River* (1939). Her last film was the mystery-fantasy *Earthbound*, released in 1940.

Leeds was admitted to a Palm Spring hospital on April 8, 1984, in the last stages of cancer. She died on May 21, 1984.

The March 27, 1938 edition of the *Montana Standard* proudly announced in advance of the day's showing of *The Goldwyn Follies* at the Rialto Theater that the country's newest film star in Hollywood "is a native of Butte" and "is going places in film": "Andrea Leeds is a young lady who knows what she wants—and what she doesn't want, it is said in Hollywood. As a result of that admirable quality, she is being hailed as Hollywood's most important new acting find."

Butte-born Andrea Leeds was nominated for an Academy Award for Best Supporting Actress in *Stage Door* (1937). *Courtesy Butte Archives.*

WILLIAM "BUD" LUCKEY

Born July 28, 1934, Billings, Montana

Bud Luckey's drawing career started during his childhood in Montana. "When I was 4 years old I used to draw on the sidewalk with broken brick," Luckey told *Entertainment Weekly* in 2011. "My big thing was before World War II I would draw Hitler and Mussolini and Tojo. And all the kids would gather round to spit and stamp on them....That's when I learned how to win friends and influence people."

His craze for cartooning was nurtured by Billings Senior High art teacher Earl Bailey. "If it wasn't for him [Bailey], I wouldn't be where I am." Luckey said. "That's why I'm bothered when people talk about doing away with art programs in school." Luckey sent an annual Christmas card to Bailey for many years.

Bud Luckey created his Senior High mural, *Canyon Creek Battle*, in 1953, and it is still displayed there. It was drawn from his memories of his grandmother's homesteading days north of Laurel, near the Canyon Creek Battle site.

Luckey attended the Chouinard Art Institute in Los Angeles, where he studied with several animators of classic Disney films. Later, at USC, he was taught by Art Babbitt, the animation director of *Pinocchio* and *Dumbo*.

Luckey worked briefly on the first *Alvin and the Chipmunks* cartoons and made short films for the first season of *Sesame Street* before he joined Pixar in 1992. He finished his art career with Pixar as a character designer for *Toy Story*, *Boundin'*, *Toy Story 2*, *A Bug's Life*, *Monsters, Inc.*, *Finding Nemo*, *Cars*, *The Incredibles*, *Ratatouille* and *Toy Story 3*.

At age sixty-nine, he was nominated for his first Academy Award—writing, directing and singing in the animated short *Boundin'* (2004). Luckey wasn't the first Montanan to end up as an accomplished illustrator. Butte-born Don Griffith (1918–1987) moved with his mother and siblings to Hollywood as a young boy after his father died. His mother ran a boardinghouse in Hollywood. When he was nineteen, Don got a job at Disney Studios on Hyperion Street in Los Angeles as an inker. He worked his way up to layout, background and art director. Don worked at the studio for fifty-two years, excepting a stint with the Merchant Marine during World War II.

DAVID LYNCH

Born January 20, 1946, Missoula, Montana

David Lynch remains Hollywood's most inscrutable auteur. The director has made a career of marrying the macabre and the mundane, never more successfully than in 1990's *Twin Peaks*, the phantasmagorical cult TV drama about a small-town murder that became a national obsession and spawned countless imitations. *Twin Peaks* was the recipient of significant media attention in 1989 and made "Who Killed Laura Palmer?" one of the urgent questions of the year.

Lynch first achieved cult status as a film director with *Blue Velvet*, a lurid, voyeuristic film steeped in violence and cruelty, one of the most controversial films of 1986. Both of these projects are situated in small towns of the Pacific Northwest.

Other important Lynch directorial efforts include *Eraserhead* (1977), *The Elephant Man* (1980), *Dune* (1984) and *Wild at Heart* (1990).

Lynch was born in Missoula in 1946, and he moved around the Pacific Northwest until he was fourteen, when the family relocated to Washington, D.C. His father was raised near Highwood, Montana, on a wheat ranch, and his grandfather was a state senator in Montana.

Lynch's *Blue Velvet*, which many Missoulians suppose is based on events that took place at the historic Wilma building, features Kyle MacLachlan in an odd love triangle with Isabella Rossellini and an uncannily deviant Dennis Hopper. The film earned Lynch a Best Director Academy Award nomination.

Lynch told the *Missoula Independent* that he lived in Missoula for two months. Lynch dismissed the rumor circulating in Missoula for years that *Blue Velvet* was based on a historic building in Missoula similar to the apartment building in the film. "Unfortunately, no," said Lynch. "There's no connection....I was born there, and right after I was born my parents moved to Sandpoint, Idaho. I lived in the Northwest until I was 14, but always in different cities....My relatives in Montana were in Hungry Horse, Montana; my aunt and uncle lived there. My parents have a log cabin up near Kalispell....They retired from the ranch and lived in Hamilton for a while. I've been to Montana a lot, but never really back to Missoula."

When he returned to Montana, Lynch said that he "mostly heads back to the Kalispell area" and that he had no memories of Missoula at all: "But

I've heard people say it's a great town and I should go visit it because it's got a real mood. And I want to go find the hospital I was born in and see if it brings back memories. I remember it was two miles from Hell's Canyon… St. Patrick Hospital. That's it. I'd like to get back there."

Lynch directed and premiered his *Twin Peaks* sequel, which reunited several leading cast members, on Showtime in 2017.

Other Montana-born directors include Billings-born John Dahl (neo-noir genre) and Great Falls–born Jerry Molen, who appeared in supporting roles or cameos in several of the films he has produced, including *Rain Man*, *Days of Thunder* and *Jurassic Park*. Molen produced five of Steven Spielberg's films and won an Academy Award for co-producing *Schindler's List*.

IAN MACDONALD

Born June 28, 1914, Great Falls, Montana
Died April 11, 1978, Bozeman, Montana

Ian MacDonald will always be remembered as Frank Miller, the fierce killer set to arrive in Hadleyville at high noon to take revenge on young, fresh-faced sheriff Gary Cooper in Fred Zinnemann's epic *High Noon* (1952).

McDonald was born Ulva William Pippy on June 28, 1914, in Great Falls, Montana. The name Ulva is an ancient Norse derivative loosely translating to "wolf island." His father, William Pippy, was a Methodist minister who homesteaded in the Havre area. His mother was born in Canada as Sara Ann MacDonald.

Born in New Foundland, Reverend Pippy came to Montana in 1910. He held pastorates in the Montana conference at Chester and Shelby before World War I.

In 1916, Reverend Pippy served as chaplain in Company C of the 163rd Montana Infantry Regiment, 41st Division, on the Montana border. At the outbreak of World War I, he was appointed chaplain of the noted Montana regiment by Governor Samuel V. Stewart. From 1917 to 1919, he was in France with headquarters at Mont Richard and St. Aignan.

Reverend Pippy came to Helena in 1925 to become chaplain at Fort William Henry Harrison, where he served for twenty-five years. He also occupied pulpits in churches at Clancy, Marysville and Wolf Creek during his many years in the ministry. He had three sons and a daughter.

During his school years, young Ian was athletic, playing high school football and basketball, yet still expressing an early interest in drama. After graduating from the small parochial Intermountain Union College in Helena, where he served as president of the drama club, Ian worked at various jobs: clerk in a bank, on a highway construction gang and schoolteacher in the virtual ghost town of Marysville, where he was superintendent, repairman and taught all high school classes. In the 1930 U.S. Census, Ian lived at 400 Harrison in Helena with his family of seven.

He started his theatrical career with the Helena Little Theater. The May 9, 1934 edition of the *River Press* finds an advertisement for the religious play *The Rock*, presented at the church auditorium on May 12, 1934, by members of the dramatic club of Intermountain Union College of Helena, under the direction of Miss Elsie Lundborg of the dramatic department. The cast included Ulva Pippy, who, like every member of the cast, was a member of a national dramatic society.

After moving to California, he studied at the Pasadena Playhouse. Ian entered films as a villain in a pair of Hopalong Cassidy films in 1941. MacDonald struggled in small, often uncredited roles for the next several

Character actor Ian MacDonald started his theatrical career in the 1930s with the Helena Little Theater. *Courtesy Montana Historical Society.*

years. He eventually cemented a career by beating out a number of quality actors for the choice role of Frank Miller in *High Noon*.

MacDonald is credited with serving in the armed forces during World War II, explaining the gap in his film credits from mid-1942 through 1946. United States World War II army enlistment records cite his enlistment date as January 14, 1942.

By the mid-1950s, Parkinson's disease had begun to have an effect on MacDonald. He lacked mobility in his right arm and nursed it in various scenes.

The world premiere of Warner Bros.' *Montana* provided Helena picture fans a chance to see home talent when McDonald, aka Pippy, arrived in the capital city to see the premiere on January 10, 1950. He played the part of the villain in the picture. The premiere featured the appearance of other Hollywood stars, including Alan Hale and Alexis Smith, who played the lead in the picture, which depicted the war between the sheepmen and cattlemen during the early period of Montana's history.

Ian was one of the featured players in the 1955 film *Timberjack*, based on a story by Dan Cushman of Great Falls. It was filmed in western Montana and Glacier National Park. Director Joseph Kane and Republic Pictures production company made Missoula, Montana, its headquarters for location shooting. The company's workday started at 4:00 a.m., when cast and crew were transported some 130 miles. Some of the most breathtaking shots were made around St. Mary Lake in Glacier National Park. The selected sites ranged from Anaconda Copper Mining Company's camp in the Poison Lake area to isolated mountain forests, made accessible by bulldozing roads through the wilderness.

Ian also worked as writer, producer, associate producer or actor in a number of movies in the 1950s, and he continued to vacation in Helena and visit friends and relatives, often making personal appearances at places such as the Old Brewery Theater.

MacDonald continued to work until 1959, when he and his wife, Shirley Kannegaard Pippy, returned to their Montana roots. The July 23, 1964 edition of the *Independent Record* previewed the *High Noon* reenactment and the city's celebration of its founding one hundred years before. Pippy was a special guest at the reenactment, which kicked off at midday with the sounds of gunshots.

Pippy was living in Bozeman when he died on April 11, 1978, of cardiac arrest and the late stages of Parkinson's disease. He is buried at Wilsall Cemetery in Wilsall, Montana.

HOWARD MCCROREY

Born September 26, 1913, Boyes, Montana
Died November 18, 1985, Hudson, Wyoming

Boyes, Montana's Howard Stanley McCrorey appeared in several productions in the 1940s as an actor, including *Trail Street* (1947) and *Return of the Bad Men* (1948). McCrorey seemed to have lived an adventurous and rugged life, although biographical details are scant. Born in southwestern Carter County, there are numerous references to him as a "Deadwood rodeo performer," and South Dakota was listed as his home state when he was inducted into the National Cowboy & Western Heritage Rodeo Hall of Fame in 1984. Photos of McCrorey on the death memorial website Find-a-Grave include intimidating images of him posing as a boxer, on the ground as a navy officer in Okinawa, socializing and drinking beer while wearing a native headdress and in action as a rodeo performer. He married his second wife in Glendive in 1954.

JOHN "JACK" MCHUGH

Born May 25, 1913, Deer Lodge, Montana
Died January 13, 1983, Las Vegas, Nevada

Born in Deer Lodge in 1913, former child star Jack McHugh appeared in more than two hundred juvenile comedies, including the Buster Brown, Big Boy and Jack McHugh series. One of the original members of the *Our Gang* comedy shorts, he appeared in such films as *Chinatown Nights* with Wallace Beery (1929) and *The Mayor of Hell* (1933) with James Cagney. Some of the other most notable films that McHugh appeared in include *Dirty Hands* (1924), *Oh, Teacher!* (1924) and *Dragon Alley* (1925).

JOHN McINTIRE

Born June 27, 1907, Spokane, Washington
Died January 30, 1991, Pasadena, California

Born in Spokane, Washington, John McIntire grew up in Montana, where his father, a lawyer, "knew many Indian leaders and where the son learned to ride broncos and love the Old West," according to his obituary in the *New York Times*. He completed high school in Santa Monica, California, studied for two years at the University of Southern California, saw the world as a seaman and learned acting on radio, yet he maintained ties with Eureka all his life.

In the 1930s, long before Montana became a popular retreat for show business stars, McIntire and his wife, Jeanette Nolan, an actress whom he married in 1935, maintained a log cabin in the Rockies three miles from the Canadian border and "14 miles from the nearest mail drop."

When one film magazine dropped in on the couple in their western Montana retreat, the writer described the last bastion of human freedom:

> *There they watched the stars through a skylight in the roof, fished for trout off the back porch, bagged an occasional bear or deer for food, trapped beavers (whose fur became a coat for Miss Nolan) and weathered temperatures of 55 below zero. She baked her own bread, churned her butter and in one year, she said, put up 500 quarts of vegetables, fruit and venison. When the couple needed to replenish their capital—Mr. McIntire said all you needed in Montana was a $200-a-year grubstake—they would come to New York and star in radio programs.*

McIntire was heard on dozens of radio's highest-rated shows and seen in more than one hundred films and myriad roles, often playing law officers, detectives, retired wagonmasters and politicians in films.

In the mid-1950s, McIntire moved into television, appearing in secondary roles in anthology series, sitcoms and dramas. He guest-starred as Judson in the episode "Chinese Invasion" of NBC's one-season western series, *Cimarron City*, with Montana native George Montgomery. According to one biographer, he "bowed out of the television show Naked City in 1959" after only twenty-six episodes and "was reluctant" to sign his *Wagon Train* contract in 1961 "because of his love for his native Montana."

143

John McIntire was heard on dozens of radio's most remembered shows and seen and heard in more than one hundred films and nearly a thousand roles.

He and his wife tried to spend six months of every year "at their primitive, untrammeled ranch where he was raised by a father who was an attorney, an Indian commissioner and an early conservationist." They often appeared onscreen together in television dramas, and Nolan once played Ann Rutledge to her husband's Abe Lincoln.

McIntire also appeared in more than fifty films in a career that nearly spanned six decades, including *The Asphalt Jungle*, *Psycho* and *Rooster Cogburn*, working alongside the likes of John Wayne, Henry Fonda, Jimmy Stewart and Elvis Presley.

Born in Los Angeles in 1911, Nolan made her film debut in 1948, and she performed in well over twenty films, including *The Man Who Shot Liberty Valance* (1962), an adaptation of a book written by Whitefish author Dorothy Johnson. Nolan was last seen onscreen as Grandma Ellen Booker, the mother of the character played by Robert Redford in the mostly Montana-made *The Horse Whisperer*. On television, where she earned four Emmy nominations, Nolan appeared on more than three hundred programs.

Their son, Tim, also an actor, died in 1986 when he was forty-two.

McIntire died on January 30, 1991, and Nolan died on June 5, 1998. Both McIntire and Nolan are both buried at the Tobacco Valley Cemetery in Eureka.

Donna Lee O'Leary

Born January 17, 1930, Butte, Montana
Died April 3, 2011, Santa Clarita, California

A child musical prodigy, Donna Lee O'Leary, the daughter of Mr. and Mrs. John O'Leary of 605 West Mercury Street in Butte, was the subject of considerable favorable comment from an early age. One of five children, she had been singing since she was three years old. At age five, she signed a five-picture contract with Republic Studios. The nine-year-old soprano, who cried on a Major Bowes *Amateur Hour* broadcast in New York City "because she was homesick for Butte," once told the *Dillon Tribune* that she would rather sing than eat. At age ten, the Butte girl had won new honors in New York, winning first place for "her wonderful voice and her dramatic ability" in the RCA television contest. Later, she appeared on several radio programs, including *A Date with Judy*. She appeared in bit roles in several films in the 1930s and '40s, including in *Bedlam* with Boris Karloff in 1946.

Christopher Parkening

Born December 14, 1947, Los Angeles, California

The recordings of one of the world's preeminent virtuosos of the classical guitar, Christopher Parkening, have received two Grammy nominations in the category of Best Classical Recording.

Growing up in Los Angeles, Parkening began playing guitar at eleven. On the advice of his uncle, studio guitarist Jack Marshall, his parents bought him a classical guitar and recordings by Segovia. Duke Parkening, formerly a professional clarinetist, pushed his son hardest toward music.

Parkening created the guitar department at the University of Southern California in 1969 when he was only twenty-two, and he was serving as the head of the department when he first retired from public performance at age thirty.

In the summer of 1977, Parkening, accompanied by his wife, Barbara, waved goodbye to the performing life, with his intent of putting his career as a touring performer behind him. His idea of retirement meant primarily fly-fishing in Montana, where he agreed to found a guitar department at Montana State University and teaching a few classes. (He was awarded an Honorary Doctor of Music from Montana State University in 1983.)

"I was more or less burned out of hotel rooms, and concert halls, and airplane travel," said Parkening. "And we were turning down about two hundred dates a year. I guess as a footnote, I've always loved the out-of-doors, the mountains, the country, and in particular fly-fishing for trout. I thought thirty would be a good age to retire. I was asked to start a guitar department at Montana State University, which I did, but, apart from a small amount of token teaching that I did there, I didn't play the guitar at all for about four years."

Endless snow and winter, though, broke his spirit. "Having always seen Montana as a land of blue-ribbon trout streams in summer and autumn," said Parkening, "with rising fish and with green leaves on all the trees over beautiful green meadows, I was unprepared for the change of seasons."

During a drive to the Rosebowl game in Pasadena, California, on January 1, 1979, for the first time, he wondered if he had made the right decision to move to Montana. "We started out early in the morning, driving carefully because it was eighteen below zero with solid snowpack on the pavement in Bozeman. By the time we reached West Yellowstone, the bank marquee said it was fifty-one below zero. When a dog ran across the street, I wondered how he could survive." "Only by God's grace," he said, was Parkening able to reestablish a major concert career. Soon after, he made the decision to purchase a small townhouse in the suburbs of California and permanently relocated to L.A. a few years later.

It was in Montana where Parkening began reexamining his priorities and pondering life's big questions. He listened to taped sermons by California

Classical guitarist Christopher Parkening was awarded an Honorary Doctorate of Music from Montana State University in 1983. *Courtesy Christopher Parkening.*

It was in Montana where Christopher Parkening began reexamining his priorities and pondering life's big questions. *Courtesy Christopher Parkening.*

preacher John MacArthur and became a devout Christian. His next recordings explored spiritual themes. A performance with Kathleen Battle on a Grammy Awards broadcast and a solo recital at the Ronald Reagan White House were among Parkening's many new high marks.

In 2006, he established the prestigious Parkening International Guitar Competition, held at Pepperdine every three years. In 2012, Parkening announced that he was ending his performing career, and these days he is focused on his work at Pepperdine and family life.

A star in honor of Parkening can be viewed on the sidewalk outside the Ellen Theatre in Bozeman.

JEAN PARKER

Born August 11, 1915, Deer Lodge, Montana
Died November 30, 2005, Woodland Hills, Los Angeles, California

Jean Parker was born Lois Mae Green on August 11, 1916, in Deer Lodge. Her father, Lewis Green, a gunsmith and hunter, and her mother, Melvina Burch, reared eighteen children in their pioneer family, which began in Missouri and Iowa and eventually settled in Montana. Jean lived there until age ten and was adopted by the Spickard family of Pasadena,

Born in Deer Lodge, Jean Parker made eighty-three movie and television appearances in thirty-four years. *Courtesy Montana Historical Society.*

California, when both her father and mother were unemployed during the Great Depression.

Parker made eighty-three movie and television appearances in thirty-four years and once said, "Acting is truly a glorious profession. When anyone can give other people a few hours of escape, or enchantment, away from the ills of the world and their own personal lives, well, that's a very worthwhile occupation."

Parker played characters ranging from ingénues to country girls, in heavy drama to comedy. She toured and played on Broadway (*Dream Girl, Born Yesterday*) and coached young performers in Southern California. She was married four times and had one child. A few of her films include *Little Women, Limehouse Blues, The Texas Rangers, Deerslayer, Those Redheads from Seattle* and *Stigma*.

"I shall always love my part in 'Sequoia,'" she told *Newsweek* in 1975, "because it is the most delightful and unusual role I can ever hope to play. I have always loved animals, and the experience of starring with a deer and a puma has proved the most attractive offer of my career—(I hope my leading men will forgive me)—to say nothing of the months spent in the most picturesque districts of America, far from the maddening crowd."

KENNETH PATTERSON

Born August 3, 1911, Bozeman, Montana
Died February 16, 1990, Los Angeles County, California

Bozeman-born Kenneth Gordon Patterson ended up in Hollywood and secured small roles in several films, including *Outrage* (1950), *Invasion of the Body Snatchers* (1956), *Being There* (1979) and Al Pacino's awkwardly titled courtroom satirical drama *...And Justice for All* (1979).

SAM PECKINPAH

Born February 21, 1925, Fresno, California
Died December 28, 1984, Inglewood, California

"Bloody Sam" Peckinpah was a maverick Academy Award–nominated screenwriter and director known for films like *The Wild Bunch*, *Straw Dogs* and *The Getaway*. The rebellious, hard-living Peckinpah lived in a three-room suite at the Murray Hotel in Livingston from 1979 to 1984.

While actors Peter Fonda, Jeff Bridges and Margot Kidder resided outside Livingston, it was actor Warren Oates who brought Peckinpah to Montana in 1976. Oates owned about six hundred acres in the mountains on Six Mile Creek near Emigrant, where he had built a cabin. He was having trouble making the payments and offered to sell half of the land to Peckinpah, who could build a cabin of his own there.

Paranoid and prone to extended bouts of cocaine binging, Peckinpah had taken over an entire floor of Livingston's venerable Murray Hotel because he was afraid to spend time at his cabin. "It was very sad, that meeting in Montana," Albert Ruddy recalled in the book *Bloody Sam*. "He was living in this second-rate hotel and it was like something out of a bad Western. He was walking around at the hotel in flannel pajamas, a bathrobe and slippers, looking very pale."

During his period of what one author describes as "psychosis" in Livingston, Peckinpah, still living at the Murray Hotel, went to a justice of the peace and got married for the fourth time in January 1980. The marriage to Marcy Blueher lasted a month. While he loved the idea of the cabin, he wasn't as enamored of actually staying there as he thought he would be. In Livingston, Peckinpah spent much of his time living at the Yellowstone Motor Inn and the Murray Hotel. On May 15, 1979, Peckinpah was in his room at the Yellowstone Motor Inn when he suffered a heart attack. Peckinpah would require an extended hospital stay, as well as a heart pacemaker. After spending two weeks at Livingston Memorial Hospital, recovering from the operation and from delirium tremens, according to one of his biographers, "he returned to the Murray Hotel and continued to drink and use cocaine. The Murray suite—with its burglar alarms and grated windows, its hiding places for drugs and cash—became a paranoid's bunker."

According to *Bloody Sam*, his daughter, Kristen, was invited to visit Livingston in January 1979 and was alarmed at what she found. "Peckinpah had not been sleeping, driving himself with a steady intake of alcohol and cocaine. Emaciated and gray-skinned, he had haunted eyes and was talking about government conspiracies. He was sleeping with a loaded shotgun in his bed, with the muzzle pointed toward his head."

Livingston's Joe Swindlehurst, Peckinpah's friend and attorney, got the director out of trouble with the local law. "There were a group of college students staying with him in his cabin," said Swindlehurst in the book. "One of them said Sam went berserk and attacked him with a pistol because he was sleeping in Sam's bed. They claimed Sam had brandished a pistol and Sam said they'd attacked him with a knife. They had him arrested, but he got off."

He was pronounced dead of cardiac arrest at 9:45 a.m. on December 28, 1984, two months shy of his sixtieth birthday. His will left his property to his children: the ranch in Montana, his trailer and a few paintings that he had invested in that he still owned. But the paintings—three Picassos, a Paul Klee and a Matisse drawing—were sold to pay taxes. So was most of the acreage in Montana. Peckinpah's children and the heirs of Warren Oates ultimately settled their debt by ceding five hundred of the six hundred acres on which the cabins were situated to the U.S. Forest Service. The Peckinpahs and the Oateses each got to keep their cabin and about fifty acres.

"Most of his violence was pure theatricality," author Thomas McGuane once told a biographer of Peckinpah. "But he was a terrible human being— depressed, angry, and with a serious drug problem."

One can rent the suite Sam Peckinpah called home—with its living room, dining room, kitchen, two-tiered bar (one level for drinking, one for arm-wrestling), two bedrooms and two baths—for $180 per night, while regular rooms start at $65.

JOE PHILLIPS

Born May 12, 1913
Died October 19, 1972

Montana-born Joe Phillips started acting in 1935 as a party guest in *Hop-a-Long Cassidy* (1935). Among the most popular movies in his filmography are *Angel and the Badman* (1947), *Rio Bravo* (1959) and *The Music Man* (1962). His television credits are equally impressive, a stroll through the dozens and dozens of icons of the 1940s, '50s, '60s and '70s, including *Bonanza*, *Kung Fu*, *Gunsmoke*, *Alias Smith and Jones*, *Here Come the Brides*, *The Guns of Will Sonnett*, *Hondo*, *Cimarron Strip*, *The Virginian*, *The Big Valley*, *Daniel Boone*, *Death Valley Days*, *Wagon Train*, *The Fugitive*, *Rawhide*, *The Dakotas*, *The Rifleman*, *Lawman*, *Have Gun—Will Travel*, *Bat Masterson*, *Stagecoach West*, *Wanted: Dead or Alive*, *Zane Grey Theater*, *Maverick*, *The Twilight Zone*, Walt Disney's *Wonderful World of Color*, *Zorro*, *Frontier Doctor*, *Mackenzie's Raiders*, *Playhouse 90*, *Tales of Wells Fargo*, *Cheyenne*, *Stories of the Century*, *The Cisco Kid* and *The Lone Ranger*. Among fans of western programs, Phillips is most remembered for his appearances in four episodes of *The Rifleman* as a townsman. In his final role in the 1973 television movie *The Night Strangler*, he played a detective.

MARLIZA PONS

Born February 9, 1936, Sidney, Montana
Died May 2, 2011, Las Vegas, Nevada

Famous belly dancer Marliza Pons was born in Sidney, Montana. Her mother, Charlotte Espinosa, was a Shoshone Indian born on the Wind River Indian Reservation in Wyoming in a teepee, and Charlotte grew up on the Northern Cheyenne Indian Reservation in Montana.

Charlotte's own mother died from stomach cancer when she was only about six years old, leaving her, her little sister and little brother. They were immediately put in an orphanage in eastern Montana with the nuns who, according to a close friend of Marliza's, "were extremely cruel to them."

"That's why there are no enrollment records for them," said her close friend Rossah Bendahman, "because her mother was gone and she [Charlotte] had been taken away. She slaved to care for her siblings and ate lard and cheese when they weren't watching because she was so hungry. When she was getting a little bigger she would clean for other people."

Charlotte Espinosa worked the fields in eastern Montana, where she met her future husband, Juan Partida, a migrant field worker from Mexico. Charlotte later divorced Juan and eventually moved to Chicago from Montana, leaving her son, Daniel, with his grandfather and taking her two girls, Maryanne and Marliza.

Famous belly dancer performer Marliza Pons was born in Sidney, Montana. *Courtesy Rossah Bendahman.*

In addition to her roles in a few films, the strikingly glamorous Marliza Pons developed into an iconic figure in American belly dancing. *Courtesy Rossah Bendahman.*

In addition to her roles in a few films, the strikingly glamorous Marliza developed into an iconic figure in American belly dancing and helped to shape the face of Las Vegas with her many dance revues, belly dance conventions, concerts and school of dance. Marliza passed away on May 2, 2011, in Las Vegas, of an aortic aneurysm, aged seventy-five.

CHARLEY PRIDE

Born March 18, 1938, Sledge, Mississippi

Charley Pride has lived the life of a legend; his prelude to fame was stamped with a Montana pedigree. "We spent seven and a half years in Helena, and then two and a half years in Great Falls," said Pride. "It was about a month short total of 10 years in Montana. I believe it was from April of 1960, to when we left in 1969. My two youngest were born up there. I'm blessed with a good memory, going back 50 years."

Pride was born March 18, 1938, on a sharecropping cotton farm in Sledge, Mississippi. At age fourteen, Pride purchased a guitar from a Sears Roebuck catalogue and taught himself the riffs he heard on country music radio. Music, however, took a backseat to his dream of becoming the greatest professional baseball player who ever lived. Pride pitched for several minor-league teams in the Negro Leagues throughout the mid-1950s before serving two years in the U.S. Army.

Following service, he returned to baseball. After three games with the Missoula Timberjacks of the Pioneer League, in 1960, he was released. Dejected, Pride followed a tip that there were a few semipro teams in Helena. He immediately found work at construction sites.

Within days of his arrival, postmaster and baseball manager Kes Rigler showed up at Pride's YMCA room and offered him a chance to play for the East Helena Smelterites and also a job at the American Smelting and Refining Company (ASARCO).

Pride was a pitcher and outfielder on the Smelterite team and batted a State Copper league–high .444 in his first season.

Realizing that Helena could turn into a long-term residence, Pride made arrangements for his wife—in 1958, he married Rozene Cohran while playing baseball in Memphis—and young son to join him. Charley and

Charley Pride's music career began in Montana in 1960 during a time when he played professional baseball for teams in East Helena and Missoula. *Courtesy Charley Pride.*

Rozene lived in Helena from 1960 to 1967. They first rented an apartment on Fifth Street and then at 825 Madison Avenue, apartment no. 1. Rozene worked as a technician at the Hawkins-Lindstrom Clinic in Helena.

At seventy-six, Pride's memories of the dust and danger of the smelter linger. He once broke his ankle on a slope of craggy pocketing, and years after he left, he heard rumors that one of the men he'd worked alongside burned to death on the job.

"I would unload the cars, and I'd send the coal up to feed down into the furnace," said Pride. "It was 2,400 degrees. It would get the nickel and gold out of the slag, and process the zinc out of it. My job was to keep the mouth of the furnace open, so it could breathe. When you were done tapping the slag out of the furnace, you would take it to the hill and dump it. You wore glasses, and it would fry your skin. You would still get just a little bit on you, it would hit you on the arm, or up above the glove."

While living in Helena, Pride earned tryouts for the California Angels (1961) and New York Mets (1965), but they declined to sign him. Pride then turned to playing more in the local bars and entertained at a number of ASARCO picnics held at McClellan Creek. "I would work at the smelter, work the swing shift and then play music," said Pride. "I'd work 11-7. Drive. Play Friday. Punch in. Drive. Polson. Philipsburg."

After work, Charley played at various saloons and pubs, frequently solo, and other times as part of a four-piece combo called the Night Hawks.

The Prides settled at 638 Peosta, a few blocks west of Carroll College. Two of Pride's three children were born in that house (his oldest son was born in Colorado when he was in the army). On March 23, 1962, a son, Dion, entered the world, and later, on April 18, 1965, Angela arrived. Both were born at St. Peter's Hospital.

Chet Atkins at RCA heard a demo tape of Pride's and signed the vocalist in 1966. Later that year, Pride's debut single, "The Snakes Crawl at Night," was released. "I always hear a rumor that there was no photograph because I was black," said Pride. "But that's not true. My biggest problem was that promoters were afraid to bring me in. But people didn't care if I was pink. RCA signed me, and all of the bigwigs, they knew I was colored, but unanimously, they decided that we are still going to sign him. They decided to put the record out and let it speak for itself."

Released at the end of 1966, the song "Just Between You and Me" began a streak of successful singles that eventually led Pride into the Country Music Hall of Fame. Only Elvis Presley sold more records for RCA.

In the mid-1960s, Pride's engagements and bookings flourished. "I started recording in Helena, but I couldn't get to a plane fast enough," said Pride. "I needed a place to fly to and from my dates, so we moved to Great Falls. In Great Falls, I still sang. I got a job on 10th Avenue South at a club, and put a band together."

Pride befriended a Great Falls businessman and native Texan named Louis Allen "Al" Donohue, who is often credited with giving Pride his start. Donohue, who was the majority owner of the Heritage Inn and the Budget Inn and co-owned KMON and KNUW radio stations, began sending the record to different stations.

Pride said that he and his wife returned a few years ago to Great Falls, and while looking at their former rental house, they bumped into the present owner. "We pulled up and there was the fellow who was living there now, he was getting ready to back out," said Pride. "We didn't move, so he would have to get out and say something. I said, 'I want my house back,' and laughed. He took us through the house again."

Reflecting on the 1960s, Pride remembered only the good, the formative days and friendships, the hard work and hope of tomorrow. "Montana is a very conservative state," said Pride. "I stood out like a neon. But once they let you in, you become a Montanan. When the rumor was that I was leaving, they kept saying, 'We will let you in, you can't leave.'"

Occasionally, Pride drops in on his old town and residence. When the UBC store in Helena was built in 1982, Charley attended the grand opening. He took photos of the house in 2005.

In 2000, Pride received word that he would be formally inducted into the Country Music Hall of Fame in Nashville, Tennessee, becoming the first black American to receive this honor. Living in Dallas, Texas, decades and millions of miles haven't dislodged Pride's recollections of Montana or his undeviating affection for the people, towns and cities where he literally found his rhythm and, perhaps most importantly, made a family.

"I will always think of that house on Peosta when I think of your state," said Pride. "That was our little darling. Always love seeing it."

WARD RAMSEY (JOHN DOANE SUTPHEN JR.)

Born September 24, 1924, Helena, Montana
Died December 24, 1984, San Bernardino, California

John Sutphen was born at 19 Jefferson Street in Helena in 1924, and after graduating from high school in 1940, he worked as a messenger for the Helena Western Union office until joining the Marine Corps in 1942. He served with distinction as a pilot in the South Pacific, according to one of his film bios, "flying between eighty and one hundred missions bombing Japanese positions in the Bismarck Archipelago." Upon his return to Helena, he served as a sergeant in the Montana National Guard and worked for a period as a policeman, bartender, sales manager at the Chrysler dealership and, finally, manager of the Montana and Green Meadow Country Clubs.

Bored of his job at the Montana Club and with the connections of some club members, he was able to "secure a position with the New York-based Harkrider Agency, working as a male model from late 1957 until 1959." According to one of his later film bios, "Sutphen appeared in magazines like Life and Saturday Evening Post and sold Dial Soap, Libbey Crystal, DeBeer Diamonds, Alpine Cigarettes and Carter Hall Pipe Tobacco and shampoo."

In 1959, the agency sent him to Mount Hood to film a television commercial for Alpine Cigarettes, which reinforced Sutphen's image as a

Ward Ramsey's sole starring role occurred as the film's hero and romantic lead in Universal's *Dinosaurus!*, a 1960 science fiction film directed by Irwin Yeaworth. *Courtesy Ramsey-Sutphen Family.*

hardy outdoorsman and stirred the imagination of Universal-International Studio. The studio, which was seeking a replacement for Jeff Chandler, who was then in ill health (he died in 1961), asked Sutphen to test for a role in film opera *Black Orchid*. Although he failed to receive the part, he signed with Universal and received the sum of $1,600 per week.

Studio publicists changed his name to Ward Ramsey, and he appeared in at least nine films, including *Pillow Talk* (1959), with Doris Day and Rock Hudson, and as a police officer in the original *Cape Fear* (1962) with Gregory Peck and Robert Mitchum.

His sole starring role (originally intended for Steve McQueen, who starred in *The Blob*) occurred as the hero and romantic lead in Universal's 1960 science fiction thriller *Dinosaurus!*, directed by Irwin Yeaworth.

A Universal publicity department release compared Ramsey to Jeff Chandler, Rock Hudson and Tony Curtis. Sutphen was quoted as saying, "Hollywood is supposed to be the land of glamour, but so far I've never worked so hard in my life!" Reviews, such as this one in the *New York Times*, were less than stellar: "MOTION picture art hit rock bottom all over town yesterday with the arrival of 'Dinosaurus!' on the circuits....If ever there was a tired, synthetic, plodding sample of movie junk, it's this 'epic' about two prehistoric animals hauled from an underwater deep-freeze by some island engineers."

In a 1995 interview, Yeaworth stated that "Ramsey was a nice-looking guy, much better in stills than he was in the movie, and he was a good guy....We got along fine, even though he wasn't ready for this." Although *Variety* panned the film, the trade paper felt that Ramsey, who purportedly told family members and friends not to see the movie, deserved a second chance.

That second chance eluded him; he played only bit parts in subsequent movies, including an extra in Marlon Brando's political flop *The Ugly American* (1963).

From the late 1960s until 1975, he worked for the Niagara Chair Company, was a car salesman in Hollywood and, after 1975, a public relations man for the Western Bass Association. In 1984, John D. Sutphen Jr., or Ward Ramsey, died of pancreatic cancer at age sixty in Encino, California. His son, John Randolph Sutphen, appeared in several low-budget martial arts action films in the 1990s under the pseudonym Chase Randolph.

MARTHA RAYE

Born August 27, 1916, Butte, Montana
Died October 19, 1994, Los Angeles, California

Behind the huge smile and raucous laugh, Martha Raye was indeed a multifaceted personality with an assortment of names to match her temperamental disposition. Her birth name was Margy Reed, and the stories she told of her birth in the mining town of Butte, Montana, must have been true because each time she spoke of her parents and the date she was born, August 27, 1916, the details were consistent.

Raye's mother, Maybelle "Peggy" Reed, was born in Montana to Teresa Sanchagrin and Samuel Hooper, who worked as a smelter in Great Falls. Samuel was born in Michigan to English immigrants. Raye's father, Pete Reed, had Irish relatives who still worked back home in the mines of County Clare. (Maybelle adopted the stage name Gertrude Sutton and appeared in several films throughout the 1920s and '30s.)

As the story goes in Butte lore, the manager of the Maguire Opera House was not impressed by the vaudeville team of The Girl and the Traveler (Maybelle and Pete, that is), who came into his office in August 1916 and pleaded for a job.

According to one Raye biographer, "He stared at the nineteen-year-old girl, who looked ready to give birth any day, and at her older, debonair husband. Just another down-on-their-luck pair, he must have thought, striking out on their own and traveling what seasoned performers called the 'sudden-death circuit.'"

The manager supposedly shrugged when the fast-talking Pete Reed boasted of how he and his wife recently had packed in audiences that overflowed into the aisles back in "Frisco." Here in Butte, the manager told them, they ran a tough schedule of four shows a day.

Still, the Reeds looked as if they desperately needed a job, and the manager relented. On that August evening of 1916, when the Reeds bounced out onto the opera house stage, they were introduced as an "Irish immigrant team."

By 1900, the population of Butte had zoomed to thirty thousand. Butte had become one of the ugliest, wildest towns in the West, and at

The daughter of vaudeville entertainers, Martha Raye was born in the mining town of Butte, Montana, on August 27, 1916. Within days, her parents had moved on elsewhere beyond Montana. *Courtesy Butte Archives.*

the end of their nights, grimy miners crowded into Butte's saloons or jammed into the opera house, stamping their boots and applauding.

Both Peggy and Pete anticipated getting paid for their performances in Butte so they could pay for the downtown furnished room they had rented in Uptown. They also needed money for food and a doctor's services. When Peggy's faint labor pains began, Pete hurried to the opera house. There he discovered that the manager had skipped town with the box office receipts.

Pete Reed had no choice but to take his wife to St. James Hospital, where she was admitted "as a charity case." Peggy endured hours of hard labor, and the baby girl's name was recorded on her August 27 birth certificate as "Margy Reed." Two days later, Peggy tucked her daughter into a basket backstage and then danced out onto the platform with her husband.

According to her autobiography, "They were back on the circuit again, riding the Anaconda and Pacific to Deer Lodge and moving, with baggage and baby (and soon even more babies), to perform their routine on any makeshift stage in any raw, western town as they gradually worked their way to the Midwest."

By the 1950s, Margy Reed had become Martha Raye and was hosting her own highly rated television show, reaching millions with her clowning. Her rowdy, slapstick comedy got her onto *Milton Berle's Texaco Show*, *The Steve Allen Show* and *The All-Star Revue* and led to her own *Martha Raye Show*. She was hailed as the country's number-one comedian for the 1953–54 season.

She was passionately committed to entertaining troops abroad during World War II, and she worked tirelessly as both entertainer and nurse in the remote jungles of Vietnam. Bob Hope commented that "she was Florence Nightingale, Dear Abby, and the only singer who could be heard over the artillery fire." The Green Berets designated her an honorary lieutenant colonel, and she later received the Presidential Medal of Freedom. Raye received special presidential praise and a special 1969 Academy Award for her morale-boosting entertainment of troops in Vietnam.

There was a darker side to Raye, who found solace from her insecurities and a frenzied schedule in the use of drugs and alcohol. Her seven rocky marriages, the last to a man thirty-three years her junior whom she had known less than two weeks, fueled headlines and gossip columns.

Toward the end of her life, Raye lived in California and had a number of projects, including feature films and stage work. She spoke five languages and enjoyed deep-sea fishing, interior decorating and reading. After her death in 1994, "Colonel Maggie" became the only civilian laid to rest among the Green Berets at the Fort Bragg military cemetery.

STEVE REEVES

Born January 21, 1926, Glasgow, Montana
Died May 1, 2000, Escondido, California

Steve Reeves's parents met and married in Scobey. When he was only months old, Reeves won Healthiest Baby of Valley County, the first title in a lifetime of awards.

Steve's father, Leslie Reeves, was born on May 10, 1899, at Winona, Minnesota, and came to the Richland community of Montana in 1916, "where he soon became known as a likeable hard-working fellow." Goldie Boyce became Mrs. Leslie Reeves.

Leslie "was a fine figure of a man," and folks in the Richland community were shocked when a threshing rig accidentally drove a pitchfork into his stomach, resulting in a painful death for the twenty-eight-year-old. It took Leslie five days to die, and he was transported to three separate hospitals. Steve was less than two years old at the time of Leslie Reeves's accident. Leslie was buried at the Scobey Cemetery, and Steve, who spent his summers in Montana on his uncle's ranch, would return throughout his life to visit his dad's grave.

During the Great Depression, in 1932, Steve's mother, Goldie, found work as a cook at the Rainbow Hotel in Great Falls. Because there was no one available to see after her six-year-old son, Steve was sent to the Montana Deaconess School in Helena. In his 1995 book, *Building the Classic Physique the Natural Way*, Reeves recounted his experience in Helena. He wrote that "over the next three years" he only got to see his mother "once a month, and sometimes during the summer." In October 1935, legendary earthquakes struck the Helena area. During the month, three big booms and thousands of tremors took place, causing $4 million in damage and killing four people. The Deaconess was ruined, which Reeves chronicles in his book.

"As it hit in the morning, all of us were sleeping in our beds," he wrote. "My dormitory was on the third floor of the brick building…and everyone went running outside.…The outside wall of the room was gone and they found my bed—with me still sleeping in it—hanging out about a foot through the opening and covered with fallen bricks (Hey, I've always been a sound sleeper, what can I say)," Reeves wrote.

Steve's mother and kids moved to California in the mid-'30s when Steve was ten. He joined the army after graduating from high school and

Steve Reeves's films weren't commercially successful in the United States but reportedly did very well in Europe and other countries around the world.

served in the Philippines during World War II and in Japan afterward. Returning to the Yarick gymnasium in 1946, Reeves soon began to win bodybuilding titles, beginning with Mr. Pacific Coast in 1946 and 1947. In 1947, he was named Mr. America, and in 1950, he won the "Mr. Universe" title.

Bodybuilding titles brought him to the attention of Hollywood filmmakers, including Cecil B. DeMille, who convinced Reeves that "he might have a future as an actor, with the proper instruction," so he moved to New York and studied with various teachers.

At age twenty-one, Reeves was six-foot-one, 215 pounds, with an eighteen-inch bicep, a fifty-one-inch chest and a twenty-nine-inch waist. His first film, made in Rome in 1957 by director Pietro Francisci and called in Italian *Le Fatiche di Ercole* (*The Labours of Hercules*), was to launch a box office genre for the Italian cinema, much as with spaghetti westerns a few years later. Like many of his films, it wasn't commercially successful in the United States but reportedly did very well in Europe and other countries around the world.

Reeves was one of the highest paid actors in Europe at the time, appearing as Hercules, Aeneas, Phillipides and Romulus in a sequence of low-budget gladiator films. In his roles as Hercules and other cinematic heroes, he was able to do almost all of his own stunts, particularly those involving horses. This was of great advantage to directors, as Steve's unique proportions made finding a double difficult.

Montana bodybuilding champion Troy Bertelsen formed a lifelong friendship with Reeves. In 1988, Bertelsen started his own gym in Whitefish, with Reeves helping with the grand opening. Bertlesen spent the latter part of the 1990s in the movie industry in Los Angeles, working at Reeves's ranch between jobs. Once when Reeves visited Whitefish, he borrowed the Bertelsen's car and racked up three thousand miles on it, visiting his relatives in Havre, Hamilton, Big Sandy, Scobey and Lewiston.

Reeves passed away on May 1, 2000, due to complications from lymphoma. His final wishes were fulfilled when, after cremation, part of his ashes were spread over the Big Snowy Mountains and the rest were buried two years later at the Scobey Cemetery, next to his father, Leslie. The headstone, which is chiseled with a poem written by Steve, was paid for by the profits from Bozeman's WFNA Big Sky Natural Physique Classic, which was organized by Bertelsen.

CHAN ROMERO

Born July 7, 1941, Billings, Montana

Born in Billings in 1941, recording artist Chan Romero cemented his rock-and-roll legacy as the author of "The Hippy Hippy Shake," which he originally recorded in 1959, hitting the national charts in the early part of 1960.

"The Hippy Hippy Shake" found a place in the history of international popular music after the Swinging Blue Jeans had a big hit with the song during the British Invasion year of 1964. The Beatles also recorded Romero's song on two different occasions. In 1988, "The Hippy Hippy Shake," performed by the Georgia Satellites, was featured in the Tom Cruise motion picture *Cocktail*.

Romero said that after he watched Elvis on *The Steve Allen Show* in 1956, everything in his universe changed. As has often been remarked of charismatic figures, such as the fictional James Bond or the real-life Presley, women wanted to be with him—men just wanted to be him. "Before Elvis," John Lennon is said to have remarked, "there was nothing." Romero said that he identified with Lennon's statement.

"Elvis came out and it was the first time people had seen him," said Romero. "I heard him sing 'Hound Dog' on *The Steve Allen Show*. He was the new American sensation, and it blew me away. I watched it on a black-and-white television bought from Sears and Roebuck, and I wanted to learn guitar then."

Romero, age seventy-seven, lives in California and still performs his signature song at festivals and events worldwide.

MERCEDES SHIRLEY

Born January 6, 1926, Billings, Montana
Died January 29, 1999, Sherman Oaks, California

Mary Mercedes Shirley was born in Billings and most known for her small roles in television programs, although she did appear on the big screen in B movies. Among her Broadway credits were *Desperate Hours* with Paul Newman and Karl Malden, *Heartbreak House* with Beatrice Arthur and *The Father* with Raymond Massey and Grace Kelly. She also appeared in stock stagings of *A Streetcar Named Desire* with Dennis Weaver and *Period of Adjustment* with Robert Vaughn. Shirley appeared in numerous TV roles in the 1950s, '60s and beyond, on such shows as *Playhouse 90, Bonanza, The Twilight Zone, Father Knows Best, Mod Squad* and *Trapper John, M.D.*

MICHAEL SMUIN

Born October 13, 1938, Missoula, Montana
Died April 23, 2007, San Francisco, California

Michael Smuin, the son of Safeway butcher and market manager Harold Smuin, was born in Missoula, Montana, on October 13, 1938. As a child, he took tap and ballet lessons but refused to wear tights. He won a letter in boxing as a high school freshman.

Michael's parents were active in the community theater in Missoula. His mother, Shirley, was an actress, and Michael's earliest shared memories include family Christmas parties with Missoula relatives, plus his passion for the dancing of Gene Kelly and Fred Astaire, his movie idols. He wanted to dance like them and was serious in attending tap dance classes at a young age.

According to an article in a San Francisco magazine, "At the age of eight he was a member of The Wise Guys, a group of youngsters who sang, tapped, and told jokes for such groups as the Chamber of Commerce, Kiwanis Club, and Red Cross." When Ballet Russe de Monte Carlo came to town in a one-night stand, Michael became an instant convert to ballet.

At twelve, he began tap lessons with Pauline Ellis at her school in Missoula, earning money to pay for his classes by doing odd jobs around town. He studied weekly for three years.

Encouraged by his parents, he spent several summers in Salt Lake City studying ballet, and then for his last year in high school and two years in college, he studied ballet at the School of the San Francisco Ballet.

At fourteen, he qualified to study dance at the University of Utah, where he was spotted by the director of the San Francisco Ballet. He began dancing

THE WHITE HOUSE
WASHINGTON

November 25, 1969

Dear Mr. Smuin:

The splendid performance of "Fancy Free" you
and your colleagues in the American Ballet
Theatre gave at the White House last week was
a highlight of our State Dinner for Prime
Minister and Mrs. Sato. I am sure that all
who were present will long remember the beauty
and skill captured in your art and would agree
that it represented a superb musical moment by
some of the world's finest dancers. Mrs. Nixon
and I were delighted that you could be with us
and I want to express my thanks to you once
again for the generous gift of your time and
your talent.

With my best wishes,

Sincerely,

Richard Nixon

Mr. Michael Smuin
American Ballet Theatre
1619 Broadway
New York, New York   10019

Missoula-born choreographer and dancer Michael Smuin received this letter from President Richard Nixon in 1969, praising the entertainer's sense of craft. *Courtesy Montana Historical Society.*

with that company in 1953, at fifteen, and moved rapidly up the ranks to become a principal.

In 1961, he was drafted for army training. By that time, he had become leading dancer of the San Francisco Ballet, its ballet master and its resident choreographer. Discharged from the army in 1962, he returned to San Francisco, where in 1966 he joined American Ballet Theater (ABT) and toured with the ABT until 1973, before becoming co-artistic director of the San Francisco Ballet.

Sophisticated Ladies brought him the 1981 Outer Critics Circle Award and two Tony Award nominations, one for choreography and one for direction.

In 1982, Smuin was one of seven award recipients presented with specially designed medallions at the Montana Governor's Awards for the Arts program of recognition.

Other awards include two Emmys, one for choreography and one for direction, for *A Song for Dead Warriors*, nationally broadcast in January 1984. He was head choreographer for several films, including Francis Ford Coppola's film *Cotton Club*.

For his choreography for the Lincoln Center's *Anything Goes*, the 1988 revival of the Cole Porter musical, Smuin received a Tony Award, a Fred Astaire Award and the Drama Desk Award.

Smuin died in 2007 in San Francisco at age sixty-eight after suffering a heart attack.

Tap dancer Gregory Hines said in 2007, "Michael's special. He recognizes at once the accent and rhythm required for theatricalization, and surprising for someone of his intensity, he's patient, very patient. No hysterics. Multi-talented, he knows what he wants and he works for it.'"

HAILA STODDARD

Born November 14, 1913, Great Falls, Montana
Died February 21, 2011, Weston, Connecticut

Haila (pronounced "*hay*-luh") Stoddard was born prematurely at a train station in Great Falls, Montana, on November 14, 1913, and was thought to have died. Her parents, Canadian Mormons, were on their way to Salt Lake City. She was named for the nurse, Haila Hahn, who, according to Stoddard's obituary in the *New York Times*, "rescued her from a waste basket with the cry, 'Doctor, it's alive!'"

The family lived in Salt Lake City until Haila was eight, when the family moved to Los Angeles. She graduated from the University of Southern California. Her producing career began in earnest in 1953, when she was acting in summer stock at the Elitch Theater Company in Denver; her off-Broadway producing credits included *Lemon Sky*, a 1970 family drama by Lanford Wilson that starred Christopher Walken and

Charles Durning; and *Love*, a 1984 musical lampoon of marriage that starred Nathan Lane. According to *Playbill*, Stoddard was "an unusual Broadway artist who transitioned from actress to producer during a lengthy theatre career."

CONSTANCE TOWERS

Born May 20, 1933, Whitefish, Montana

Constance Towers was born in Whitefish, the daughter of Ardath L. Reynolds and pharmacist Harry J. Towers, both Irish immigrants. In 1940, when Towers was in first grade, she was discovered by talent scouts visiting Montana in search of child actors for radio programs. She then worked as a child voice actress in Pacific Northwest–based radio programs for three years. According to her website, Towers was offered a contract with Paramount Pictures at age eleven, but the offer was declined by her parents. At age twelve, she worked at a small local movie theater in her hometown of Whitefish. In her adolescence, her family relocated to New York City for her father's work. Although a veteran of a number television and film roles, Towers's best-known part is as villainous Helena Cassadine, a role originated by Elizabeth Taylor, on *General Hospital*, which she began playing late in 1997, continuing on and off ever since.

JACK WALRATH

Born May 5, 1946, Stuart, Florida

Jack Walrath started playing the trumpet at the age of nine in 1955 while living in Edgar, Montana, a tiny speck of a town with the population of one hundred that has since become a virtual ghost town. He developed "a healthy perception of music from lack of negative peer pressure which so often happens in cities," according to one interview with Walrath in 2001. In 1964, after graduating from Joliet High School in Montana, he attended the Berklee College of Music, graduating in 1968 with a degree in composition. Walrath's talents have been utilized by Charles Mingus,

Ray Charles, Miles Davis, Elvis Costello and a host of other notables. He has appeared in films, television and radio as a sideman and leader since 1965. He has released twenty-two record albums as a leader and has appeared on countless albums with some of jazz music's great icons, including fourteen times with Mingus. His Blue Note album, *Master of Suspense*, was nominated for a Grammy in 1986.

HAZEL WARP

Born November 11, 1914, Harlowtown, Montana
Died August 26, 2008, Livingston, Montana

Born in Harlowton in 1914, Hazel (Hash) Warp earned her place in cinematic history when she served as actress Vivien Leigh's stunt double as Scarlett O'Hara in the epic film *Gone with the Wind*. A Sweet Grass County native who became a rodeo trick rider in her teens, Warp stood in for Leigh in all the horseback-riding scenes in the 1939 Civil War movie.

According to her obituary in *Western Horseman*, "Hazel Hash grew up on a small farm near Melville, attended a one-room schoolhouse and rode horses whenever she could, always bareback. She quit school after ninth grade, started training horses and wound up on the rodeo circuit."

In her twenties, she followed her older sister to California "on a whim, taking the Greyhound bus all the way," she once said in an interview.

Her sister and brother-in-law ran Rancho Rio Stables in Culver City, where they raised and trained champion horses and "gave riding lessons to the likes of Elizabeth Taylor, Grace Kelly and Gary Cooper." Montana-born cowboy-actor Montie Montana helped Hazel get into the film business, where her equine proficiency was sought after by directors. She also appeared in *Wuthering Heights*, *Ben Hur* and *National Velvet*, among others.

Her work was honored in 2001 with a star in front of the Rialto in Bozeman.

DOROTHY WHITE

Born September 22, 1911, Butte, Montana
Died October 11, 2008, Sun City, Arkansas

Butte-born Dorothy White appeared in several pictures in the 1930s, including *42nd Street* (1933) and *Gold Diggers of 1933*. In a career that spanned from 1931 to 1940, White appeared in forty-three productions as dancers and checkroom, village and nightclub girls. She died on October 11, 2008, in Sun City, Arizona.

BETTY WONDER

Born August 25, 1912, Havre, Montana
Died July 24, 1979, Sacramento, California

Born in Havre, Betty Wonder moved to California at age young age with her mother and adopted brother, Tommy. While Tommy had a long successful career as an actor, choreographer and professional dancer, Betty had a less memorable career as an actress, appearing in smaller roles in films such as *Varsity Show* (1937) and *The Wages of Sin* (1938). She died on July 24, 1979, in Sacramento, California.

TOMMY WONDER

Born March 7, 1914, Havre, Montana
Died December 11, 1993, New York City, New York

A native of Montana, Tommy Wonder grew up in California and started dancing when he was three. An adopted child, he and his sister, Betty, were put on the vaudeville stage by their mother, Tillie Wonder, when her husband died not long after the adoption.

Tommy was one of the children in the Our Gang comedies and went on to work as an actor in pictures as well as a dancer onstage. He was a principal dancer in the *Ziegfeld Follies* of 1943, a version of the Follies that turned out to be one of the most successful. The cast was led by Milton Berle and Ilona Massey, and Wonder's partner was Nadine Gae. He and Berle were among the few principals who stayed for the complete fourteenth-month run.

Among his film credits were *Gangster's Boy* with Jackie Cooper (1938) and *Thrill of a Lifetime* (1937) with Betty Grable and Dorothy Lamour. When he stopped appearing on the stage in 1970, he turned to managing as a partner in Tommy Wonder & Don Dellair Artist Management, on Madison Avenue. Dellair was the singer in a trio that also featured Maggie Banks, Wonder's dancing partner and at one time wife.

Wonder and Dellair went on a world tour with Josephine Baker and then starred in the French extravaganza *Avec Frenesies* at the famed Casino de Paris Music Hall in Paris for three years.

In 1993, Wonder died of heart failure at Cabrini Medical Center in New York City. He was seventy-eight and lived in Riverdale, the Bronx.

IRENE YEAGER

Born December 15, 1912, Montana
Died February 28, 1999, San Juan, Washington

Yeager was an actress, known for *The False Code* (1919), *The Way of the Strong* (1919) and *The Jack-Knife Man* (1920). She died on February 28, 1999, in San Juan, Washington. A review of the film *Breaking Point* in the August 13, 1922 *Anaconda Standard* referred to Yeager as "the well-known child actress."

BORN AFTER 1960 AND MODERN CAREERS

PHILIP AABERG

Born April 8, 1949, Havre, Montana

Born in Havre and raised in Chester, Philip Aaberg was performing with local bands at dances at the age of fourteen. In 2000, Aaberg began Sweetgrass Music, a medium through which he has endeavored to produce music that "connects a global audience to the sweeping landscape of the West."

Throughout his career, Aaberg has composed piano music that consistently interpreted Montana's farms, ranches and native cultures into "musical concepts" and has "forged a unique keyboard style that paints an audible portrait of his home state."

Philip and his wife, Patty, operate several businesses throughout the Hi-Line area, including Sweetgrass Music, the Great Northern Bed and Breakfast, the Westland Suite and The Bin recording studio.

GARY ALBRIGHT

Born May 18, 1963, Rhode Island
Died January 7, 2000, Hazelton, Pennsylvania

Gary Albright started amateur wrestling at Billings West High School, where he had a 55-2 record. Albright was the 1980 state champion and the following year placed second in the state championships. Albright would go on to wrestle in the NCAA for the University of Nebraska, where he set the Nebraska State record for total falls in a season: thirty-eight falls in the 1985–86 season.

He made his debut as an entertainment wrestler in 1988 and soon after would participate as a talent almost exclusively for Japanese promotions focused on shoot, or unscripted aspects, of staged professional wrestling.

On January 7, 2000, Albright wrestled at a World Xtreme Wrestling show in Hazleton, Pennsylvania, against Lucifer Grimm. After being hit with a three-quarter facelock bulldog, Albright collapsed to the canvas. Albright was pronounced dead of a heart attack shortly after being removed from the ring.

The medical examiners also found that Albright, father of three, suffered from diabetes and had an enlarged heart and blockage of several coronary arteries.

Albright is not the only famous Montana connection to entertainment wrestling. John Nord started as a football player, playing offensive tackle at Montana State (1981–82) and then for the New Jersey Generals of the USFL, with Herschel Walker. Nord started wrestling in late 1984 as "The Barbarian" for Mid-South Wrestling under manager Skandor Akbar and reached the pinnacle of notoriety in the early 1990s in the World Wrestling Federation as The Viking and later The Berzerker, when he was managed by Mr. Fuji. He retired from wrestling in 1998 after suffering a neck injury. He told *Wrestling Illustrated* in 2010 about the physical troubles he has endured from entertainment wrestling. "The thing about wrestling is, it's so hard on you. You crack. You have to medicate yourself to keep going."

JEFF AMENT

Born March 10, 1963, Big Sandy, Montana

A Montanan from Big Sandy is a member of the Rock and Roll Hall of Fame. Pearl Jam, including Big Sky–born bassist Jeff Ament, were part of the 2017 class of inductees that included the late rapper Tupac Shakur, folk icon Joan Baez and 1970s favorites Journey, Yes and Electric Light Orchestra.

Ament grew up in the small town of Big Sandy and took to playing the bass and creating art. Ament attended the University of Montana, where he formed his first band. Formed in Missoula in 1982, Deranged Diction exhibited raw punk similar to the Ramones, the Stooges and the Clash. The band had moderate success before packing their bags for Seattle in 1983. After the breakup, Ament went on to join Green River, Mother Love Bone and finally Pearl Jam, which became a part of Seattle's burgeoning grunge scene. Pearl Jam rocketed to worldwide popularity with its debut album, *Ten*, which includes some of the most iconic songs of the decade, like "Jeremy," "Even Flow" and "Alive."

Over the course of ten albums and stadium tours, the band has maintained most of its original members, including singer Eddie Vedder and guitarists Mike McCready and Stone Gossard.

The group started its 1998 tour with a concert at Washington-Grizzly Stadium and have played the Adams Center three times, most recently in 2012. The band released a limited-edition bootleg of that last concert and donated the money to the Poverello Center, a homeless shelter in Missoula.

An avid skateboarder, Ament lobbied for many years to build Mobash Skate Park in Missoula and also helped fund it. In the years since, he has donated thousands of dollars to help build parks in small communities around the state. According to Pearl Jam's website, Ament has also helped build skate parks in Hamilton, St. Ignatius, Helena, Big Sandy, Glendive, Browning, Baker, Havre and Stevensville. He also has helped build parks in Pine Ridge and Wounded Knee in South Dakota.

BILL BOWERS

Born April 16, 1959, Lolo, Montana

Miming is the powerful mode of individualism that Bill Bowers was born into. "My theory is that I'm a mime because I'm from Montana," said Bowers, a fifth-generation Montanan. "Montana is the classic big, quiet place, and I came from the classic stoic Montana family. There was lots going on in my family, but no one actually discussed anything."

Add the dimension of Bowers being a gay kid in Missoula in the 1960s and it's not hard to comprehend why Bowers gravitated to an art form where reticence reigns. "That's a lot of silence to deal with," said Bowers. "It all combined inside of me."

While Bowers had a strong inclination of the mime's career path as a youngster, his relationship with one of the world's greatest practitioners of pantomime, French-born Marcel Marceau, put in motion a chain of events that has helped put Bowers on a shortlist of the greatest living mimes.

Bowers learned from Marceau that to think creatively, one must be able to look anew at what we otherwise normally take for granted. He also learned that the mime needs to perpetuate the feeling of pure contemplation and that the mime's aim should be to represent not the outer appearance of things but rather their inner significance.

Since his relationship with Marceau, who died in 2007, Bowers has enjoyed standing ovations and sold-out performances across the nation and world. Indeed, miming is the expression of Bowers's joy in labor. That labor is silence. That silence is met with a variety of responses. "It's interesting what silence does to people," said Bowers. "Often, people have very intense emotional responses. Places that are silent—churches, temples, libraries—they are places of contemplation. Miming allows things to enter you a different way. And a lot of people spend their days trying to suppress those feelings. It's a different experience to not be distracted by the world's entire stimulus."

Bowers suggests that audiences treat miming like any other artistic medium: let it express itself to you first. "In the arts," he said, "you have an interest in empathy and understanding. That comes with the territory that we are all in. And as a mime, I like to observe how people do things, and I look for stories to tell."

Bill Bowers studied under French-born Marcel Marceau, which put in motion a chain of events that helped put Bowers on a shortlist of the greatest living mimes.

He has his own take on just why the art of miming hasn't sustained in the United States the same way it has in many other countries. "It's hard to learn," said Bowers. "But more so, our culture has moved toward if you can't do it in five minutes, forget it."

Mindful of the fact that nothing in art is ever permanent, Bowers presses on with his thought-provoking skits and themes. "If I don't do it, it could literally disappear."

JEFF BRIDGES

Born December 4, 1949, Los Angeles, California

Jeff Bridges's relationship with Montana began when he was selected to play opposite Clint Eastwood in the 1974 movie *Thunderbolt and Lightfoot*; shot in forty-seven days in the summer of 1973, almost entirely in and around Great Falls, the film follows a pair of drifters who fall into friendship and criminal enterprise. Bridges received an Oscar nomination for Best Supporting Actor for the film.

"*Thunderbolt and Lightfoot* was an exciting movie," said Bridges. "I was a young guy and Eastwood was producing [along with Robert Daley], and he was giving Michael Cimino his first shot, his first directorial job. It was filmed partly in Helena, at the Gates of the Mountains, at the Snake River. I fell in love with Montana. I bought a Harley-Davidson, and there was no better place to buy a bike and ride around....It was all a wonderful experience. The light, the mountains and the people—everything just struck a chord in me."

The 1975 Montana-made film *Rancho Deluxe*, written by Thomas McGuane, tells the quaint tale of two modern-day cattle rustlers (Bridges and Sam Waterston) disconnected between a romantic past and a motorized present and the distant memories and principles of the West.

"*Rancho Deluxe* has special significance for me because I met my wife during the filming," said Bridges. "She was working her way through college, and I couldn't take my eyes off the girl waiting tables with a broken nose and two black eyes [from a car accident]. She said no. But she said that she might see me around town, though, being such a small town. We were married three years later. On one of our first dates we went along with a Realtor."

Bridges also played in Michael Cimino's finance-inflated *Heaven's Gate*—often derided as Hollywood's biggest box office disaster, a mismanaged flop that culminated in the disbandment of United Artists. The 1980 movie, based on an 1890 range war in Johnson County, Wyoming, starred Kris Kristofferson and was filmed at five sites in Glacier National Park, as well as several areas adjacent to the park, in addition to a few scenes in Idaho and Colorado.

"Toward the end of the movie, there is a whorehouse in *Heaven's Gate*, and Michael Cimino said, 'Does anyone want this cabin?' He said that the owner or whomever was going to burn it down. I numbered the logs and took them four hundred miles south to Livingston. To this day, I'm living in the *Heaven's Gate* whorehouse."

Although primarily known for his acting, in August 2011, longtime Montana resident Jeff Bridges released his self-titled debut album for Blue Note Records, produced by T-Bone Burnett. *Courtesy Jeff Bridges.*

Bridges said that his roots as a professional musician have their origins in the unplanned jam and tutoring sessions that took place on the set of *Heaven's Gate*. "We shot for close to six months on that movie," said Bridges. "During those six months, Kris Kristofferson invited a lot of his friends. On movie sets, many actors play music. Kristofferson brought Ronnie Hawkins, Stephen Bruton and T-Bone Burnett, and our down time was spent making music. Some lifelong friendships started there, and *Heaven's Gate* was really the birth of the music that came out later in *Crazy Heart*."

Since then, Bridges has gone on to become one of Hollywood's most accomplished actors, a six-time Academy Award nominee. His performance in *Crazy Heart* (2009) as Bad Blake—the luckless, alcoholic country music singer at the middle of the drama—garnered him his first Oscar for Best Actor.

In August 2011, Jeff released his self-titled debut album for Blue Note Records, produced by Burnett. He has also released a solo effort, *Be Here Soon*, on his own label, Ramp Records, and a live album, *Jeff Bridges and the Abiders Live*.

In 1983, Bridges founded the End Hunger Network, a nonprofit organization dedicated to feeding children around the world, and fights to end childhood hunger in Montana and throughout America.

Leading roles, intermittent touring, fundraising, charity work—there is always something sending Bridges off in a different direction, splintering time. "Right now, I spend a couple of months in Montana [and the rest of the year in Santa Barbara, California]," said Bridges. "I wish it were closer to 50-50. That sounds pretty good to me."

DANA CARVEY

Born June 2, 1955, Missoula, Montana

Dana Carvey was born in Missoula, the son of Billie Dahl, a schoolteacher, and Bud Carvey, a high school business teacher.

Dana's mother, Billie, was born in Casper, Wyoming, on April 2, 1926, to Thomas McDonald and Dolores Dahl McDonald and grew up in Great Falls, Montana. She attended the University of Montana until her father died and then returned home to help her mother. In 1948, she married Bud, whom she met at a college dance. They lived in Missoula and Big Timber, Montana, while Bud completed college.

The Carveys moved to California in 1957, when Bud got a job teaching in Anderson, California. The following year, Bud got a job in San Mateo, and the family moved to San Carlos. Dana attended Tierra Linda Junior High in San Carlos and Carlmont High School in Belmont and received his bachelor's degree in broadcast communications from San Francisco State University.

Dana Carvey was a longtime favorite on *Saturday Night Live* thanks to his recurring characters like the Church Lady, *Wayne's World* cohost Garth Algar (loosely based on his brother, Brad) and former president George H. Bush. (President George H. Bush liked Carvey's version of him so much that he invited Carvey to perform at the White House.)

He joined the cast of the late-night comedy series in 1986. For seven years, Carvey delighted audiences with such characters as bodybuilder extraordinaire Hans, part of the Hans and Franz duo, and impressions of personalities such as H. Ross Perot.

Carvey's Garth character successfully transitioned to the big screen in *Wayne's World* (1992). Garth was the disheveled heavy metal sidekick to his friend Wayne, played by Mike Myers, and the pair appeared together on

Wayne's cable access show. The comedy proved to be a box office hit and spurred to a sequel, *Wayne's World 2*, the following year.

In 1993, Carvey left *Saturday Night Live* and finally won an Emmy Award for his work on the show after four previous nominations.

TOM CATMULL

Born December 20, 1968, Spring, Texas

Tom Catmull's songs deserve to be heard. Indeed, the staple Missoula singer-songwriter resonates when his timbres and tones are absorbed; the deeper you listen, the more approving the experience.

Not hearing Catmull is a missed opportunity, since he's a maestro finely mincing lively songs and instruments into a flavorsome treat. His songs are imbued with stylistic nods to singer-songwriters such as Lyle Lovett, whom Catmull grew up around in the suburbs of Houston, Texas.

Not hearing Missoula singer Tom Catmull is a missed opportunity, since he's a maestro at finely mincing lively songs and instruments into a flavorsome treat. *Courtesy Tom Catmull.*

He writes straightforward lyrics and relatable material that could exist comfortably in any era. His guitar crackles with palpable force, and occasionally, the harmonica deftly slices through a tune. At this moment, Catmull juggles solo performances as well as engagements cushioned with a band (Tom Catmull's Last Resort). He's had his most success during the thirteen-year run he had with the Clerics, which included pedal steel and acoustic guitars, drums, bass and, occasionally, the fiddle. Another recent variation of Catmull's synergy was a group called Radio Static.

His collection of songs ranges from manifestoes about independence and love to much deeper, unplugged ballads reflecting the hard road of personal truth. *Entrenched* would be one word to describe Catmull's link to the city of Missoula's music scene. Missoula's bona fide folk-country-rock swami performs at least 150 engagements per year, and he can be seen and heard at breweries, clubs, festivals and events statewide, sitting back, a master *in situ*, unfurling melodies and savoring every note. He breathes energy and spirit every time he leans toward the microphone. We're lucky to watch the throne.

"I want to take what's inside me, and I want it to be out there and inside other people's heads, and to affect people. I love to be at the right venue, with a decent guitar, choosing a good song for a good moment, connecting with people, guessing what they might respond to."

Other contemporary Montana singers and songwriters and entertainers include Jenn Adams, guitarist Steve Albini, Britt Arnesen, Eden Atwood, soprano opera singer Judith Blegen, David Boone, Almeda Bradshaw, John Dendy, Luke Dowler, John Dunnigan, Jeni Fleming, John Floridis, glam metal rocker Janet Gardner, Susan Gibson, Jack Gladstone, Andrea Harsell, Coty Hogue, Larry Hirshberg, Jessica Kilroy, Marco Littig, Amy Martin, Russ Nasset, Izaak Opatz, Erik "Fingers" Ray, Richie Reinholdt, Martha Scanlan, trumpet player Allen Vizzutti, David Walburn and Rob Quist.

SHANE CLOUSE

Born June 28, 1973, Missoula, Montana

Shane Clouse stops to enjoy his contentment and to share it. The Missoula-based musician/farmer/business owner's identity isn't some big mystery. He's just whoever he has to be to get through and enjoy the day.

With four records to his credit as well as collaborations with Grammy-winning songwriters, Missoula crooner Shane Clouse is a character who crackles with energy. *Courtesy Shane Clouse.*

With four records to his credit, as well as collaborations with Grammy-winning songwriters, the crooner within is a living, breathing character who crackles with energy. His down-to-earth decency and rugged sincerity shine the brightest in the dark corners behind the microphone.

But there is another part to Clouse, and that is his operation of the Pink Grizzly Greenhouse and Nursery, a family business of plants, vegetables and seasonal trees and wreaths, established in 1956.

He has worked hard to nurture several careers simultaneously. "I feel that Montana allows us to live and lead a very meaningful life," he said. "I wouldn't want to be a husband, a farmer, a musician, or a businessman anywhere else. In Montana, we've learned how to work harder. I've worked in England, Canada, Mexico, Australia, and people are enamored with Montana, and they recognize that we work harder here."

The youngest of eight children, Clouse recognized early that he would probably live and die enmeshed in some type of musical identity. Indeed, he began his performing career, he said, as a toddler. He would sing buoyantly to his parents and siblings "on the fireplace hearth" of the family's farmhouse. He entered, and won, his first singing competition at age five.

If his parents groomed him with a healthy dose of self-sufficiency, it was an innate sense of self-empowerment that led Clouse to polish his singing, dancing, acting and instrument playing. Following college at MSU and several stints in corporate America, Clouse has become a country kingpin in Montana. Usually accompanied by a band known as Stompin' Grounds, Clouse has opened for, among others, Clint Black, Dierks Bentley, Michael Martin Murphy, the Nitty Gritty Dirt Band and Marshall Tucker. (Formed in 2004, Stompin' Grounds still retains its original guitar and bass players.)

A happy life must be to some degree be a quiet life, for it is only in an atmosphere of quiet that actual joy subsists (or at least that's Clouse's Montana-centric spin). He was raised by his mom and dad to explore freely—and he did. Clouse, who sojourned in Nashville in the summer of 2000, returned to Montana in 2005 in search of the quiet atmosphere of his youth.

"I led a conventional life for eight years, and I left a $50,000-a-year job to make much less, to work the family business for $8 an hour. I thought it was better to make less money to pursue my dreams. It's all OK. I'm just as happy talking about tomatoes as I am about music."

THE DECEMBERISTS

Colin Meloy discovered early on that music can offset the mundane aspects of life. Heavily established in Portland, Oregon, the Decemberists' beginnings are wrapped up and enfolded in—and indebted to—the remarkably odd and furiously energetic music scene of the late 1990s in Missoula.

> *I attended the University of Montana between 1996 and 1999. So, it's the place where I started playing at open mics at coffee shops around town, and we put together* [the indie rock band] *Tarkio and we played at Jay's Upstairs* [currently the Loft of Missoula] *and the Top Hat and the Old Post, and the musical scene then was super vibrant, and the punk scene incredible. There was the Sputniks, the Volumen, Oblio Jones and others. We were playing some stuff that was different—sadder music, I think. Then* [the psychedelic-punk band] *Fireballs of Freedom went to Portland and you could just feel the exodus of music out of Missoula in the summer of 1999.*

Meloy is the son of Claudia Montagne and Mike Meloy and grew up in Helena. His grandfather Pete was a potter who joined arts patron Archie Bray in launching the Archie Bray Foundation. Pete's brother, Hank, was a painter who taught art at Columbia University in New York.

"There was always an emphasis put in the home on following your bliss," said Meloy. "That emphasis shot through me. Although, I think my parents wanted us to do it [the pursuit of art] as a hobby and not as a main goal. After all, my great-uncle died impoverished in New York becoming an artist. But my older sister [author Malie Meloy] and I definitely proved them wrong."

Hence, the blissful sounds of music served as flashy, funny, inspiring baubles. The first two records he ever owned came from Henry J's: the eponymous *Chicago 16* and *Cargo* by Men at Work, a birthday present from his mother. "There was Henry J's for the older crowd out on [the west side of town] on Euclid and Pegasus Music at the mall," said Meloy, forty-two. "Pegasus had the major label releases and an import section of CDs. Before the Internet, I had an uncle who lived in Eugene, Oregon, who would send mixed tapes in the mail. For years, Cactus Records, in Bozeman, and Rockin' Rudy's, in Missoula, provided a lifeline. Growing up, Helena was interesting because even though it was the capital, it felt like the kind of a community

The Decemberists' front man, Colin Meloy, is a Helena native who organized and headlined a multi-day music event in the summer of 2017 as a means of exposing more Montanans to various music scenes.

that you wouldn't associate with as a town in Montana of its size. It had a progressive scene and art scene."

Music was both an allure and an escape for Meloy, and at the time, Helena offered several places to escape to (although no record store exists there today). The guitar's voice was capable of expressing opinions and feelings in ways that words neglected. It dazzled and empathized. It calmed, excited and explained. It moved him.

Experimenting with the guitar had been the entry ticket into the world of wonder. Better yet, the guitar had the ability to make his life by and large better.

Music fit the kid who I was. When I hit my early teens, I didn't fit in with the interests of my peers, or interests elsewhere. I was not into sports or that world, and I loved writing. I grew up in a progressive household that was good and supportive. I loved music that felt weird in the context of local Helena radio and weird in the context of what other kids were listening to. In junior high school, I discovered and I threw myself into music that was a little more obscure than what was available at Pegasus Records at the mall. I started searching out and treasure hunting and finding this music.

I liked listening to the Smiths, the Replacements, Morrissey and Paul Westerberg. It was all of the music that had the feeling of being kind of off the mainstream, on the margins. I had a lot of feelings of being out of place and feeling like I didn't fit in, and that stuff was a real haven for me, and allowed me to get through the harder times during my teenage years.

Subsequently, Meloy cultivated a vocal style of grandeur, sensuous richness and emotional exuberance, paying homage to a worldly-wise perspective.

Meloy organized and headlined a multi-day music event in the summer of 2017 as a means of exposing more Montanans to various music scenes. "It drove me crazy how many national touring bands skipped Montana altogether. I'm glad we can do our small part to bring more music to the area. Helena and Missoula were the hubs of the state, but growing up it was slim pickings and wishful thinking as far as live music....Every tour cycle I play at least once here—much to my booking agent's chagrin."

JASON DESHAW

Born April 3, 1981, Plentywood, Montana

Born in Plentywood, Montana, on April 3, 1981, singer-songwriter Jason DeShaw was diagnosed with Bipolar I disorder as a young man and started writing songs that captured some of his struggles, attempting to frame the issue as universal. His song "Crazy Town" expresses the dreamlike moments he's had in his search for meaning. "I've been called crazy in a world that's not quite sane."

The National Alliance on Mental Illness (NAMI) noted DeShaw's advocacy work, and in September 2014, he was honored during the national convention in Washington, D.C. DeShaw was awarded the Lionel Aldridge Champion Award and praised for "exhibiting courage and leadership" as he deals with mental illness. DeShaw partnered with Blue Cross Blue Shield for a ten-city Montana tour in 2015, "Serenity in the Storm." The tour stopped in five rural communities and five bigger towns, including Billings. It featured DeShaw speaking, performing music and listening empathetically.

"It both drains the cup and fills it," said DeShaw. "After one show, I had five people come up to me who lost someone to suicide. You can't just passively listen to something of that nature. You have to commit your eyes, your attention and your soul. I've been humbled to have been put on this journey of advocacy."

STACY EDWARDS

Born March 4, 1965, Glasgow, Montana

The daughter of a U.S. Air Force officer, Glasgow native Stacy Edwards appeared in a number of B movies before a larger role in the 1997 black comedy *In the Company of Men*. Edwards later earned roles in films such as *Primary Colors* (1998), *Black and White* (1999) and *Driven* (2001) and was a regular cast member in the CBS medical drama series *Chicago Hope* (1997–99).

TROY EVANS

Born February 16, 1948, Missoula, Montana

Troy Evans's plan was to attend the University of Montana, become a lawyer, work in the state legislature, become a senator in the mold of Mike Mansfield and then represent the West in the White House. His grandfather, also named Troy Evans, was a state senator for Silver Bow County who served as state boxing commissioner under four governors.

Instead, he flunked out of college, started a college rock band, was drafted, spent two years in the Vietnam rain forest, returned home, got shot, was arrested for multiple assaults and served almost two years in a Montana prison. His stint in Vietnam left Evans cynical, psychologically damaged, hurt, angry, ashamed and incredibly violent. Returning to Montana, he opened a bar in Kalispell.

When a man propositioned another customer's wife, Evans broke his leg and cracked his skull and then went after the victim's friend, beating him with the bar's pay phone. Evans wound up being committed to the Montana State Prison and, for a period of time, the VA Mental Hospital in Sheridan, Wyoming.

After serving his nineteen months in jail, Evans got on the GI bill and enrolled in college. One year later, he was offered a scholarship to Santa Maria's Pacific Conservatory of the Performing Arts, where, he estimates, he appeared in "40 to 60" plays in four years.

Since 1979, he has lived in Long Beach, and his credits include *L.A. Law*, *Cheers*, *Hunter* and *Night Court* on TV, as well as the film *Planes, Trains and Automobiles*. He has instead carved out an ironic niche as a movie cop, appearing as a police officer or sheriff in films including *The Black Dahlia*, *Fear and Loathing in Las Vegas*, *The Frighteners* and *Demolition Man*. With roles in more than fifty films and four hundred episodes of television to his credit, Evans is best known for his recurring role as Frank Martin, a desk clerk in the television series *ER*.

Evans discussed his lunatic trajectory with *Rolling Stone* in 2014: "One day, I was sitting in my prison cell and I thought, I bet nobody ever asks an actor if he has a felony conviction," explained Evans. "Acting was my parole plan, and fortunately it worked out."

JESSE TYLER FERGUSON

Born October 22, 1975, Missoula, Montana

Jesse Tyler Ferguson was born in Missoula to Anne and Robert Ferguson. His family moved when he was young to Albuquerque, New Mexico, where he was raised. At age eight, he decided to become an actor and joined the Albuquerque Children's Theater, where he was a member for six years. After graduating from St. Pius X High School, Ferguson attended the American Musical and Dramatic Academy (AMDA) in New York City. He is best known for portraying Mitchell Pritchett on the ABC sitcom *Modern Family*, which has earned him five consecutive nominations for the Primetime Emmy Award for Outstanding Supporting Actor in a Comedy Series.

LILY GLADSTONE

Born in 1986, Browning's Lily Gladstone is of Native American/First Nations heritage, from the Amskapi Pikuni (Blackfeet), Kainaiwa (Blood) and Niimipoo (Nez Perce) Nations. In 2017, Gladstone scored three critics awards, including an L.A. Film Critics Award, as well as a Spirit Awards nomination, for her role in the indie drama *Certain Women*. That year, she also landed a regular role in WGN America's DC Comics pilot *Scalped*. Based on the western crime comics that were published by DC's Vertigo imprint in 2007, *Scalped* bills itself "as a modern-day crime story set in the world of a Native American reservation."

WYLIE GUSTAFSON

Born June 7, 1961, Conrad, Montana

Wylie Gustafson charmingly recollects his distinguished boyhood in north-central Montana. Born in 1961, the youngest of five kids (all of whom arrived within a seven-year period), his was a close-knit, tight-bonded family. His father, Rib Gustafson, a horse veterinarian and all-around horseman, instilled in his brood a love of rodeoing and ranching.

"Conrad was my world," said Gustafson. "I grew up in that culture. And there is so much to do in this part of the country. Summer time, it was a little bit of everything, including our annual pilgrimage into the Bob Marshall Wilderness for six days on horseback, where we would go in for days without seeing another soul. We'd fish and goof off. Those are some of the most poignant memories I have growing up."

In the 1990s, Wylie yodeled commercially for companies such as Mitsubishi, Miller Lite, Taco Bell and Porsche, and by the time a fledgling company named Yahoo! contacted him, he had already been rolling his vocal cords in such a manner for five years. The session with Yahoo! in 1996 was over in perhaps fifteen minutes and in about as many takes. It seemed like any other gig until the moment Wylie heard his bellowing voice during a Super Bowl commercial three years later.

"It was kind of a shock for me," recalled Gustafson. "It started off as a regional commercial, and it became their audio logo and part of their e-mail....They were pushing these ads out there worldwide. It was quirky enough and it worked with their ad campaign and their image, and the timing was just right."

Public appearances yodeling at fairs and festivals followed, and he even emceed an amateur yodeling contest that Yahoo! brought to eight cities nationwide as part of its promotional branding campaign. While he has been writing and singing country-folk songs for decades, the Yahoo! yodel has provided him with his most notable feat.

"I've spent all of my life trying to write that three-minute classic country radio song," chuckled Gustafson, "and it's funny how life will make a fool out of you sometimes. Fame came not with the three-minute song, but with the three-note song."

MARGOT KIDDER

Born October 17, 1948, Yellowknife, Canada
Died May 13, 2018, Livingston, Montana

The second-oldest child of Kendall Kidder, a mining engineer, and his homemaker wife, Jill, Margaret Kidder grew up in raw Canadian mining towns like Yellowknife, in the remote Northwest Territories, where she was born in 1948. Stunningly beautiful as a teenager, she moved to L.A. at age eighteen and got a part as "a virginal prostitute" in 1969's *Gaily, Gaily*.

In 1996, the actress, most known for her role as Lois Lane opposite Christopher Reeve in *Superman* film series, suffered a mental breakdown that made headlines across the nation.

Lost on the streets of downtown Los Angeles, Kidder was disheveled, missing her dental work, dressed in dirty garments and huddled inside the cardboard box that served as the home of a street person she knew only as Charlie. According to *US Magazine*, "Kidder had lost some caps on her front teeth that sometimes fell out and which she cemented back in place with Krazy Glue."

Throughout the delusional episode, Kidder came to the conclusion that her first husband—novelist and longtime Montana resident Thomas McGuane—"was trying to kill me." She had divorced McGuane in 1977 after several turbulent years.

According to *US Magazine*, "Disoriented and terrified, Kidder was fixated on the idea that McGuane and the CIA were plotting to kill her because her book was powerful enough to change the world. Kidder saw agents and assassins everywhere."

After being diagnosed with manic depression, Kidder relocated to a log cabin near Livingston. After the first *Superman*, Kidder worked in films like *The Amityville Horror* and had managed to stay active primarily in television movies.

In 2005, Kidder became an American citizen in Butte—after living thirty-four years in the United States. Her sole motivation, she said, "was to protest the war in Iraq."

Kidder received her citizenship at a naturalization ceremony in Butte federal court with eighteen others from countries ranging from Australia to Belize. The ceremony included speeches, patriotic songs and an oath of allegiance. She died in 2018 at her Montana home "as a result of a self-inflicted drug and alcohol overdose."

ROBBIE KNIEVEL

Born May 7, 1962, Butte, Montana

Robbie Knievel loves wreaking his own brand of adventurous havoc. He loves whiskey. He loves a good firm drink to compose his nerves before and after a death-flouting feat. He loves the daily grind of the daredevil and the buzz of stomping in the footsteps of his eminent old man. But he now values his life and health more than he does booze. Instead of whiskey and soda, he swigs Diet Cokes in the evenings and nips mochas in the morning. The Butte-born risk taker said that he is wholly committed to sobriety following a felony DUI charge on April 21, 2015.

For a man such as Robbie Knievel, if there's not any emotional drive, it's not worth hurling into. Robbie's hook of sobriety is fueling his intense preparation. He has been riding dirt bikes to pump up his forearms, cycling straight up and down, reinforcing his muscles by working the brake with the throttle. He is lifting weights, eating vitamins and dropping excess weight in his stomach.

Robbie concedes that, not surprisingly, it was damn difficult being thrust into the silhouette of the world's quintessential daredevil performer and

Robbie Knievel embraced the same traps of an entertainer persona as did his father. He learned early that his dad, Evel, was a hardened daredevil, a performer and a marketing genius. *Courtesy Alicia Knievel.*

trying to perpetuate his legacy. Evel Knievel's showmanship, flair and disdain for death were so admired that he became a national folk hero. He died in 2007 at age sixty-nine. His health had also been undercut by years of heavy drinking; he told reporters that at one point he was consuming a half a fifth of whiskey a day, rinsed down with beer chasers.

Robbie embraced the same traps of that persona. He learned early that his dad was a daredevil, a performer and a marketing genius. He knew his old man loved the thrill, the money and the whole macho mania. All those things made him one hell of a brand.

"I remember when I was eight years old and I was doing a show in Madison Square Garden," said Robbie. "I was on a bike that was way bigger than me and I rode around. Think about it: My dad's jump was the number one rated show in *Wide World of Sports* history. It doesn't matter if you are Joe Frazier's kids, Elvis's daughter, Muhammad Ali's daughter, whoever—you cannot fill those shoes. Butte was a town of fifty-five thousand, and it had a lot of bars. I grew up drinking and with a few bar fights. In Butte, your dad wanted to take you to the bars. I quit high school. I knew what I wanted to do for a living."

Dad wasn't perfect. Evel liked to brag about his early callings as a safe cracker, bank robber, swindler and pickpocket. In 1977, he roughed up his former promoter Shelly Saltman with an aluminum baseball bat after Saltman wrote a negative book claiming that Knievel abused his wife and children and was a heavy drug user. Knievel was jailed for six months. Regardless of his foibles, Evel was groundbreaking, meaningful and, at times, enthrallingly eye-opening.

"I remember watching my dad's flapjack race and seeing him at the Moses Lake speedway," said Robbie. "My homework would pile up. We went from a trailer to all these acres and horses and a Ferrari at age twelve. I don't think I realized how famous he was until the Snake River Canyon jump. He was a self-promoter. After his toys came out, he outsold GI Joe one year. We would fly to Florida, and I would be sanding his yachts at fifteen. I'd hang out on the speedboat and yachts, and I moved out at sixteen—like an idiot."

Before he was ten, Robbie was charging tourists fifty cents to watch him hurdle ten ten-speeds on his mini-bike. Robbie embarked on his own course of rousing performances. He is an old-school jumper. He doesn't practice with a foam pit or a safety net in the backyard. He learned through the onerous debt of birthright, of being ballsy and just going for it. He uses lower ramps and hits them with the highest of speeds. He once mistimed and landed the middle of the bike so hard that it bounced him over the handlebars. He badly sprained his back. But he did the very same jump the next night—a successful, certifiable no-hander. He has overtaken barreling steam locomotives and sailed over the buildings.

"I've done about seven or eight live shows. That's pressure. Timing and pressure. If you land short you get killed. You could shift wrong one time or miss that gear going to ramp with so much momentum. You can't hesitate. You've got to have the guts to pull the trigger," said Robbie. "I have never chickened out. Where would I be? Who wants to be bounced off the pavement at eighty, ninety miles an hour? When you clear it nice and clean, it feels good. But if the bike cuts out or seizes before you leave, you are screwed, and you are dead. On this coming jump—any jump—if I hit the front of that ramp wrong I'm done."

True to daredevil form, he has made the element of facing down danger look effortless. In 1989, at age twenty-six, Robbie successfully executed the motorcycle stunt that nearly killed his father twenty-two years earlier.

Robbie cleared the towering water fountain in the parking lot outside Caesars Palace. Robbie roared his 500 Honda up a ramp, soared 150 feet across the fountain, landed on another ramp and growled safely into an underground garage.

"A lot of guys do practice jumps to get the feel of the jump. Practice? It takes away from the real thing. My lower back hurts when I get out of bed every day. Legs, back, shoulders—they are sore. Everything I've injured, it still hits me now. It all started hitting me three, four years ago. Knee surgery. Ankle injuries, torn ligaments in the knee. There are times when you try to get up the next day to go to the bathroom and you have to have someone help you."

Robbie's next step is anybody's guess, including his own. He returned to Butte in 1990s after the successful Caesars Palace jump and worked hauling logs at a sawmill. Six months later, he was gone again. He recently lived in Las Vegas.

"I am still going to be jumping," said Robbie. "I've had major knee surgery, lower back issues, lumber issues, concussions, I don't know how many of them. I've had 24, 25 broken bones. But I never broke as many bones as my dad did [purportedly 433, according to his obituary]. I like to say that I am the son of the greatest daredevil in the world."

At fifty-seven, Robbie is a top-notch showman. He is his own legend, the accomplished heir who buffed the crown of a daredevil dynasty in a dignified way. "I'm happy," said Robbie. "I believe it may take one full year to get back into the limelight. But I am going to keep the name going as long as I can. It's the most famous name on two wheels."

JEFF KOBER

Born December 18, 1953

Billings-born Jeff Kober has made a career of bringing jagged, craggy characters to life for nearly three decades.

The Montanan in Kober worked hard at raising Black Angus cattle and sugar beets, but after his erudite English teacher introduced him to literature—"especially Shakespeare"—he knew that he needed to be traveling elsewhere.

According to *Variety*, "After working at the ranch, he would sit down at night and talk with the dogs like the other cowboys; he would drink wine like the other cowboys, but no one but Kober would read Nietzsche."

Kober's intense demeanor has fit into thriller, horror and even the comedy genres, having seen roles in a list of television shows and films such as the 1980s series *China Beach*, the 2003 film *A Man Apart*, 2007's *The Hills Have Eyes II* and, most recently, AMC's mega-hit *The Walking Dead*.

Taking on the role of a mysterious man named Joe who lived by his own ethos, which has kept him alive in a post-apocalyptic world, Kober brought a villain to life in an unexpected fashion that had fans applauding his performance.

In 2007, after a lengthy and intensive period of study, Jeff became a teacher of Vedic meditation and since then has taught from his center in Los Angeles, as well as in Mexico City, Chicago, Montana, Wyoming and regularly in New York.

KOSTAS

Born April 14, 1949, Thessaloniki, Greece

On March 1, 1994, Dwight Yoakam won a Grammy at the 37th Annual Grammy Awards at Radio City Music Hall in New York for his performance as best country male vocal in the song "Ain't that Lonely Yet." The award-winning song was written by nationally acclaimed Kostas Lazarides.

Kostas, born in Thessaloniki, Greece, and raised in Billings, was a recognizable face on the Montana music scene from the mid-1960s until the late 1980s, when the singer-songwriter moved to Nashville, Tennessee. He began performing in local Billings-area bands and as a solo artist during the mid-1960s while still in high school. During the 1970s and early 1980s, he performed his unique style all over Montana. His style is characterized by a richly evocative tenor voice and expressive writing of original songs. Kostas immediately established himself as one of Music City's best songwriters, penning hits for such artists as Travis Tritt, Patty Loveless, Dwight Yoakam and the Mavericks. Another noted Kostas original is Travis Tritt's megahit "Lord Have Mercy on the Working Man." He lives in Livingston.

WALLY KURTH

Born July 31, 1958, Billings, Montana

Billings-born Wally Kurth has made a successful career out of the soap opera circuit. He is best known for his work on *General Hospital* as the second Ned Ashton, whom he has portrayed since 1993, and for his role as Justin Kiriakis on *Days of Our Lives*, a role he created in 1987 and played until he left the show in 1991, returning to reprise the role in August 2009. He also played the character of Sam Hutchins on *As the World Turns* for several months in late 2007/early 2008. Before Kurth moved to California to pursue acting, he started out as a singer, polishing his skills in the West High School Choir in Billings. In the early 1990s, he formed the Kurth & Taylor Band, recording four albums worth of original songs. He and his brother, Brian, launched a music venue called Cove Creek Outdoor Pavilion in Billings in 2017.

LANEY LOU AND THE BIRD DOGS

Unifying a four-part harmony and a vigorous musical drive, Bozeman's Laney Lou and the Bird Dogs have taken an active approach to the local and regional festival circuit. With their bounce and upbeat ballads and eager-voiced delivery, the Bird Dogs hope to stake a claim in the bluegrass/folk festival genre with their own distinctive sound and devoted fan base. With a flock of musicians who draw from a number of collective experiences in eclectic bands, the Bird Dogs have comfortably settled into the frontier of bluegrass-country music. They've invested the time it takes to build the infrastructure of a fan base with a mixture of innovative covers and swift-tempo originals.

NICOLETTE LARSON

Born July 17, 1952, Helena, Montana
Died December 16, 1997, Los Angeles, California

At the zenith of her stardom, Nicolette Larson died at age forty-five of complications from cerebral edema—a swelling of the brain—at the UCLA Medical Center, leaving behind a seven-year-old daughter. "We were truly devastated when we heard the news…it is a very sad day for music," said Graham Nash of Crosby, Stills and Nash in a press release.

Born in Helena, Larson's adult life was spent far from Montana in California, where she built a long musical career. Larson's hits included "Rumba Girl," "Fool Me Again" and "That's How You Know Love's Right."

In her twenty-plus years in the music industry, Larson released six critically acclaimed albums. She started her career singing backup for renowned artists such as Emmylou Harris, Jimmy Buffett, the Beach Boys, Willie Nelson, Linda Ronstadt, Neil Young, Christopher Cross and the Doobie Brothers. Her breakthrough came in 1978 when she recorded "Lotta Love," a song she discovered on a tape lying on the floor of Young's car. "I popped it in the tape player and commented on what a great song it was," Larson said. "Neil said, 'You want it? It's yours.'"

Larson moved from Helena with her family when she was just six months old but returned there often while she was a child to pass her summers with her grandmother Elsie Hoffman. In 1989, Larson told an *Independent Record* reporter that while growing up her parents moved often, and Helena was the "only home place I knew."

Brought up in Kansas City, Kansas, Larson was working as a waitress when a trip to San Francisco in 1973 changed her life. "I got to see Tom Waits and Commander Cody and all sorts of bands," she said in 1978. "It was great. I'd get up every morning and say, 'California. I'm in California.' It was like Mecca." She moved to Berkeley soon after that and got a job as a backup singer for a short-lived band. Next she sang backup for Hoyt Axton (who later settled in the Bitterroot Valley) for a year and then joined Commander Cody.

After moving around as a child, Larson settled permanently in California when she was twenty-one and within five years was singing the chart-topping hit "Lotta Love." She often introduced the song as a gift from Young. Larson also released six critically acclaimed albums during her career.

Born in Helena,
Nicolette Larson is
best known for her
1970s cover of Neil
Young's "Lotta Love."
*Courtesy Montana
Historical Society.*

In 1989, when she returned to Helena to perform for a hometown crowd, Larson reflected on memories from there. "I can't believe I'm playing the Civic Center," she said at the time. "I used to walk by it on my way to the swimming pool. I could never figure out the Moorish architecture." Even during concerts in other places, Larson's memories of Helena would surface, with fans hearing stories between songs of the annual painting of the "H" on Mount Helena and the once-annual MacDonald Pass picnic. During another visit to Helena in 1994, when she brought her then three-year-old daughter, Elsie, to see her great-grandmother and namesake, Larson described Helena as "the real touchstone of my childhood."

DAVID LETTERMAN

Born April 12, 1947, Indianapolis, Indiana

On May 23, 1998, talk show giant David Letterman was ticketed by a town marshal for doing thirty-eight miles per hour in a twenty-five-mile-per-hour zone in Darby. Letterman was cooperative as he paid the fifty-dollar fine. For years, Letterman made jokes about his speeding tickets on the Merritt Parkway in Connecticut during program monologues and other comedy routines. Letterman made several jokes about his speeding ticket in Montana upon his return to *The Late Show* in June.

Turns out Letterman was visiting Montana to check out real estate, purchasing a three-thousand-acre ranch in the Front Range country west of Choteau. Letterman memorably discussed his life in Choteau when addressing a shocked and saddened nation looking for answers in the days following the attacks of 9/11:

> *There's a town in Montana by the name of Choteau. I know a little something about this town. There's 1,600 people. Montana's been in the middle of a drought for three years and if you've got no rain you can't grow anything and if you can't grow anything you can't farm and if you can't grow anything you can't ranch because the cattle don't have anything to eat and that's the way life is in this town of 1,600 people....Last night in the school auditorium in Choteau, Montana, they had a rally—home of the Bulldogs by the way— they had a rally to raise money for New York City and if that doesn't tell you everything you need to know about the spirit of the United States, than I can't help you. I'm sorry.*

In an interview with the *Billings Gazette* in 2015, Letterman talked at length about his first impressions of Montana and his transition to becoming a part-time Montana resident.

"I remember coming across the Continental Divide around Lincoln and then you drop down onto the east side and we drove the Front and I thought, 'This is kind of the vision of what I had in my mind,' without knowing anything about the state....I'm not sure quite how people from Choteau feel about anybody moving in and buying land but by and large everybody has been very nice to me, celebrity notwithstanding. [My celebrity status] almost has not been a factor. It's been all good."

In 2007, he asked Willie Nelson to put on a free show for the town, and the singer obligingly played to 3,200 people. During his tenure between 1993 and 2015, Letterman even booked several of his Montana neighbors on *The Late Show*, including Great Falls resident Richard Baker as his "twin brother," Great Falls Johnny Cash cover band The Cold Hard Cash Show on as musical guests and Great Falls native Ryan Simonetti, who hopped his skateboard onto a Uhaul.

Living on the Rocky Mountain Front hasn't been without its worries for Letterman. In 2005, Simms resident Kelly Frank, who was working as a painter on the Letterman ranch, plotted to kidnap the comedian's then sixteen-month-old son and his nanny in exchange for a $5 million ransom. He was convicted and served nearly ten years.

Overall, however, he told *People* magazine that there are only two kinds of reactions from the friends he invites to Choteau to share his land with: "[T]hose who get it and love it and people who wonder, 'What the hell have you done?' Those people don't get invited back. The people who do get it do get invited back and enjoy it again and again and again. It's an interesting read of personality but not everybody does get it which I was surprised by."

HUEY LEWIS

Born July 5, 1950, New York City, New York

Singer Huey Lewis, who was raised in Marin County, California, moved to the Bitterroot Valley, Montana, in 1987 and lives on a five-hundred-acre ranch outside Stevensville, between a healthy dose of touring and other responsibilities. The crowd at the final Out to Lunch of the summer of 2015 was treated to a surprise visit by the '80s rock legend during the Big Sky Mudflaps' set in Caras Park. Lewis ripped through four R&B classics, including "Blue Monday," made famous by Fats Domino. Lewis sang lead and played harmonica. In 2013, he spoke with the *Wall Street Journal* about a fishing road trip to Montana with his friends in the early '70s during which he fell in love with that part of the country. "I never tire of the Montana lifestyle—but it's challenging. There's a lot to stay on top of out here. In Montana, everything slows down, and finding motivation requires effort. For example, we have wonderful fly-fishing, but fly-fishing takes work. There's a boat and a lot of gear involved. So I constantly try to remind myself: 'You live in Montana, man. Get out and do something every day.'"

BILL PULLMAN

Born December 17, 1953, Hornell, New York

Bill Pullman, who played a role in two Montana-made movies released in 2017, *Walking Out* and *The Ballad of Lefty Brown*, brings his own Big Sky connection to the films. Having exercised his craft in the 1980s performing and directing with Shakespeare in the Park, a theatrical outreach of Montana State University, Pullman went on to co-chair MSU's Theater department and plant roots in Montana that hold him to this day:

> *Montana Shakespeare in the Parks might have been a little different back then because of the home stays and the immersion into the community. There was no hotel to stay in, and we'd go into people homes. Eventually, the tours got longer, and it became easier to put yourself in hotels. The home stays allowed for more intimacy with people's lives, and it tied in to a good concept with community. One of the magic ingredients was the fact that the setting was with your community in the background. It was the set, the open air, the park and the community was part of the play, and that was something I enjoyed.*
>
> *There were so many memorable interactions with nature, like early in the season, when great storms are still possible, big thunderclouds. I remember once at Chico, watching the storm build behind the hills, and build up to a skyscraper, and finally, it came above, and it let loose. We had these amazing final moments as the thunderstorm crashed down. In Miles City, in a park, we were there with cottonweed trees and cotton blowing during A Midsummer Night's Dream. We were surrounded by cotton seed, and it was beautiful. In Montana, the audiences are patient and they stick around through a storm. They go get the rain gear on and wait ten, fifteen minutes until it's gone and sunny. It all worked because the audience was savvy.*

In the early 1990s, Pullman, a married father of three, bought a ranch near Cardwell.

J.K. Simmons

Born January 9, 1955, Grosse Pointe, Michigan

When it comes to incarnating depraved or evil, few actors are more qualified than J.K. Simmons, 1978 University of Montana alumnus. A forty-year veteran of stage and screen, its little surprise that his first major TV role back in 1996 was as a criminal policeman. But he never did wicked better than in his Oscar-winning performance as a sadistic music teacher in 2014's *Whiplash*.

His major at UM was music, but he did summer work as an actor at the Bigfork Summer Playhouse and eventually moved to New York City, where his acting career took off. In 2016, Simmons was the keynote speaker for the class of 2016 commencement and received an honorary doctorate degree from UM. "Be here now." Simmons summed up his advice for the graduates in those three words.

Misty Upham

Born July 6, 1982, Kalispell, Montana
Died October 5, 2014, Auburn, Washington

The Native American actress Misty Upham played alongside Hollywood's best. Born in Kalispell, a member of the Blackfeet Nation, Upham landed the role of Oscar winner Meryl Streep's housekeeper in the 2013 drama *August: Osage County*. Her success was short-lived and ill-fated. In October 2014, her body was found in a ravine in Washington State after she went missing for eleven days. Upham, thirty-two, who had battled mental illness and suffered from debilitating anxiety for years, had a "psychotic episode" the afternoon she vanished, according to her father.

Blackfoot actress Misty Upham and Benicio Del Toro in a scene from *Jimmy P: Psychotherapy of a Plains Indian*, released in 2013. The aspiring thirty-two-year-old was found dead in a ravine near Seattle in 2014. *Courtesy Montana Film Office.*

Her untimely death marked the end of a life filled with onscreen triumphs—after winning acclaim for 2008's *Frozen River*, she appeared in several movies, including 2012's *Django Unchained* and the drama *Jimmy P: Psychotherapy of a Plains Indian*, which was partly filmed in Montana.

REGGIE WATTS

Born March 13, 1972, Stuttgart, Germany

Born in Germany, comedian and entertainer Reggie Watts attended high school in Great Falls, Montana, where, he said, "I literally lived through a John Hughes movie in my time there."

"I was definitely sort of a class clown," said Watts. "With Great Falls, people either hate it or love it, for sure. I love it for a lot of reasons, the great memories, and it's where I became myself and grew up. While it doesn't have an obvious artistic culture, it was the perfect time to be there in junior high and high school. It was like *Sixteen Candles* or

Great Falls High School graduate Reggie Watts can be seen on CBS network television Mondays through Thursdays as the bandleader on *The Late Late Show with James Corden. Courtesy Reggie Watts.*

Weird Science or *Ferris Bueller's Day Off* or *Better Off Dead.* Dope music. No cellphones. Great Falls allowed me the chance to be who I wanted to be—a weirdo—and there was no bullying, and I met a lot of other weirdos and we had a weirdo club, which did art, dreamt, did music and had free rein."

Reginald Lucien Frank Roger Watts was born in Stuttgart, Germany; his mother is French, and his father, Charles, was a U.S. Air Force officer. At eighteen, the 1990 Great Falls High School graduate moved to Seattle and played in bands before landing in New York in 2004.

Watts can be seen on network television Mondays through Thursdays as the bandleader on *The Late Late Show with James Corden,* who took over the CBS program in 2017 from Craig Ferguson. *The Late Late Show* is shot four afternoons per week at CBS Television City in Hollywood.

Watts plays a lighthearted and good-natured part on the show, equivalent to Paul Shaffer, who served worthily as the sidekick for many years to talk show host David Letterman. "I think he got shown a video of mine," Watts told *Spin.* "They were looking for a musician type of cat."

Watts maintains a brisk schedule of entertaining as a beatboxer/ musician/comedian/improviser, increasingly known for his musical sets that are created spontaneously using only his voice and looping pedals. He always adds a show or two in Montana to his performance schedule, and he returns to Great Falls almost monthly to visit his mother.

"Great Falls is blue-collar and gritty and rock-and-roll, and I dig it," said Watts. "Missoula more like Nirvana and cool bands and wine and breweries building all the time and enjoy that, but Great Falls is a simplistic stereotype, and I keep it to the people who can appreciate it for what it is."

Other contemporary entertainers from Great Falls include sisters Missy and Tracey Gold, actresses best known for their roles in 1980s sitcoms *Benson* (Missy) and *Growing Pains* (Tracey).

MICHELLE WILLIAMS

Born September 9, 1980, Kalispell, Montana

Michelle Williams spent her early childhood in Montana, with her younger sister, Paige, and three older half siblings from her father's first marriage.

The family moved to San Diego when Williams was nine; her mother, Carla, took care of the children. Her father, Larry Williams, was twice the Republican Party nominee to the United States Senate in Montana. He lost in the general election both times.

As a child, she told *Variety*, "there were a bunch of kids my age that were going to L.A. to auditions, and I was just one of them. I was just kind of swept up in a tide—a little minnow swimming along."

Williams began acting professionally at eight; her first film role, in 1994, was in a remake of *Lassie*. "It seemed exciting to my parents," she told the *Los Angeles Times.* "They were from Montana; they wanted their kids to have a little bit more opportunity—every parent wants more for her kid. I think on the outside when you see your kid audition, it seems very glamorous. Then you realize it's kind of like a horrible factory that you're feeding your children into."

Williams legally emancipated herself from her parents when she was fifteen and moved to Los Angeles on her own. "All I can say is that it was a strange and bizarre choice that was bolstered by the agreement of my parents. When I think of my own daughter…I couldn't do it, I'd be so afraid. Now, when I meet 15-year-olds, I worry about them because you're such easy prey at 15."

"Living alone in a little apartment was terrible," she told *Vogue*. "I furnished it from Ikea. I didn't know how to make a home, so I slept on an egg crate on the floor, and the only thing I knew was how to make pasta, but I didn't understand portions, so I would dump the whole box of pasta in the pan, heat up an entire jar of sauce, and put melted cheese slices on top."

Since breaking into the entertainment world with a part in the television show *Home Improvement* in the early 1990s, Williams has been nominated for four Academy Awards and one Tony Award.

After a two-and-a-half-year legal battle, her father, Larry Williams, finally consented to be extradited to the United States, where he faced long-pending federal tax evasion charges. On February 5, 2010, those charges were dropped, and he pleaded guilty to three misdemeanor charges of failing to file income tax returns on time.

GEORGE WINSTON

Born 1949, Michigan

George Winston's melodious musical language won an audience with albums such as *Autumn*, from 1980, and *Winter into Spring*, from 1982. Then he won a Grammy for Best New Age Album for *Forest* in 1994. Winston plays solo guitar and solo harmonica in addition to piano. While Winston has also lived in Mississippi, Florida and California, Montana, he said, "is absolutely the basis," for much of his inspiration.

"You can the boy out of Montana, but you can't take Montana out of the boy. It's just there," Winston said. "It's like the trees in different locales come up from different places in the earth and they're that kind of tree. Musically, it's the same thing.

Born in Michigan, Winston was a small child when his family moved to Miles City, Montana, and a few years later to Billings. "We had no TV," recalled Winston. "There was one radio station. Train was the main travel, and the main entertainment was the seasons. It was baseball in the fall, swimming in the summer, building a snowman in winter, playing with leaves in autumn. Everything reminded me of a season. Not all of my albums are named after seasons, but all songs are seasonal to me."

Winston, who spent twelve years in eastern Montana, made it clear in 1994 in the liner notes to his Grammy Award–winning album, *Forest*, that the first track, "Tamarack Pines," is "influenced by the work of composer Steve Reich and inspired by the Tamarack Pines of western Montana, which are unusual in that the pine needles turn yellow and drop from the trees in the fall."

"In the early '80s, I remembered the yellow pines and even in Miles City patches of pines and Dad's company picnics as a kid. Wind through the pines."

Raised partially in eastern Montana, pianist George Winston's melodious language won an audience with albums such as *Autumn*, from 1980, and *Winter into Spring*, from 1982. *Courtesy George Winston.*

His feelings for his Big Sky home cropped up in his 1999 album, *Plains*, and even more directly in his 2004 project, *Montana—A Love Story*. Similarly, the title track to *Plains* leaves the listener no uncertainty of where that music is from—the subtitle is "Eastern Montana Blues."

BIBLIOGRAPHY

Allen, Steve. *More Funny People*. Briarcliff Manor, NY: Stein and Day, 1982.

Norman, Barry. "Gary Cooper." In *The Hollywood Greats*. New York, 1980.

O'Donnell, Monica M., ed. *Contemporary Theatre, Film, and Television*. Vol. 4. Detroit, MI: Gale Research, 1987.

Parish, James Robert. *The Slapstick Queens*. San Diego, CA: A.S. Barnes, 1973.

Slide, Anthony. *Hollywood Unknowns: A History of Extras, Bit Players, and Stand-Ins*. Jackson: University Press of Mississippi, n.d.

Smith, Bill. *The Vaudevillians*. New York: Macmillan, 1976.

Steinberg, Cobbett. *Film Facts*. New York: Facts on File, 1980.

Terrace, Vincent. *Encyclopedia of Television Series, Pilots, and Specials*. Vols. 1 and 2, 1937–73. New York: Zoetrope, 1986.

ARCHIVES AND LIBRARY SOURCES

Library of Academy of Motion Picture Arts and Sciences, Beverly Hills.

New York Times Indexes, 1935–95.

INTERVIEWS

Dirk Benedict
Troy Bertelsen
Bill Bowers
Jeff Bridges
Tom Catmull
Shane Clouse
Jason DeShaw
Wylie Gustafson
Robbie Knievel
Colin Meloy
Christopher Parkening
Charley Pride
Bill Pullman
Chan Romero
Reggie Watts
George Winston

NEWSPAPERS

Bridgeport Sunday Post. April 29, 1956.
Detroit News. February 17, 1938, and others.
Great Falls Tribune. May 10, 1960, and others.
Helena Independent Record. April 5, 1950, and others.
Montana Standard. August 12, 1980, and others.
New York Times. August 1, 1936, and others.

PERIODICALS

American Weekly. April 26, 1937, and others.
Collier's. May 1, 1937.
Etude. June 1941.
Radio TV Mirror. April 1954 and others.

Saturday Evening Post. May 7, 1955.
TV Guide. November 20, 1954, and others.
Variety. December 23, 1942, and others.

PUBLIC RECORDS AND VITAL STATISTICS (ONLINE ACCESS)

Detroit, Michigan.
Helena, Montana.
Jacksonville, Florida.

INDEX

ABOUT THE AUTHOR

Brian D'Ambrosio lives in Helena, Montana. He has written several books, including most recently *Montana and the NFL*, with Arcadia Publishing, and more than three hundred articles about Montana people, places and things. He may be reached at dambrosiobrian@hotmail.com.

Visit us at
www.historypress.com